D1367728

Additional Praise for
Follow the Fed to Investment Success

"Follow the Fed is a great resource for anyone who wants to understand more about the world of investing. More importantly, it shows them how to make more money by spending far less time and money than they do today."

—Danon Robinson
Managing Member
Toro Trading LLC

"While Doug has written this book for the novice investor, even the most experienced professional can learn from his life and investment lessons. Written in an easy to comprehend style, he mixes serious stories and advice with personal revelations and a bit of history that make this book a must read!"

Paul C. Guidone, CFA
Managing Partner & Chief Investment Officer
Linden Point Capital Management, LLC

"Doug Roberts is a superbly talented investment guru. His unique approach, proven to work in any market, allows investors to get back to their lives while beating most of the Wall Street experts. If you're looking to read only one book on growing your personal wealth, look no further that *Follow the Fed to Investment Success!"*

David N. Feldman
Feldman, Weinstein & Smith LLP

"Doug Roberts has unlocked a wonderful, simple and deeply historical perspective on how to intelligently and successfully beat the market. His well tested *Follow the Fed* model runs counter to the current 'get rich quick' investment culture, emphasizing wealth preservation and a long-term strategy."

Samuel E. Navarro
Managing Director
Cowen & Company

"Anyone who believes they'll be able to rely exclusively on Social Security for their retirement better think again. Having been a witness to years of careless government spending, I encourage everyone to find another way to ensure that you'll have the money you need to enjoy life. I have read *Follow the Fed to Investment Success,* and truly believe that this strategy has what it takes to achieve that goal."

Joe Kyrillos
New Jersey State Senator

"*In Follow the Fed to Investment Success,* Doug Roberts reduces the mind numbing financial world to a comprehensible, simple and enjoyable read. His easy to follow recommendations do not require the reader to have a Masters in Finance, nor the need to monitor the financial market for hours at a time."

Nick Brown
Managing Director
GFI Group Inc.

Follow the Fed to Investment Success

Follow the Fed to Investment Success

THE EFFORTLESS STRATEGY FOR BEATING WALL STREET

Douglas S. Roberts

WILEY

John Wiley & Sons, Inc.

Published by John Wiley & Sons, Inc., Hoboken, New Jersey.
Published simultaneously in Canada.

For general information on our other products and services or for technical
support, please contact our Customer Care Department within the United States
at (800) 762-2974, outside the United States at (317) 572-3993 or fax (317)
572-4002.

Wiley also publishes its books in a variety of electronic formats. Some content that
appears in print may not be available in electronic books. For more information
about Wiley products, visit our Web site at www.wiley.com.

Follow the Fed®, The Easy Strategy for True Wealth™, Twin Foundations™, and
The Edge™ are the Trademarks of Channel Partnership I, LLC.

Library of Congress Cataloging-in-Publication Data:

Roberts, Douglas S., 1962-
  Follow the Fed to investment success : the effortless strategy for beating
Wall Street / Douglas S. Roberts.
      p.   cm.
  Includes bibliographical references and index.
  ISBN 978-0-470-22649-0 (cloth)
  1. Investments–United States.   2. Investment analysis–United States.
3. Small capitalization stocks–United States.   I. Title.
  HG4910.R628 2008
  332.63'220973–dc22

                                                2007045608

Printed in the United States of America

10 9 8 7 6 5 4 3 2 1

Data for the Follow the Fed® strategy are drawn from several publicly available sources—U.S. Department of Labor: Bureau of Labor Statistics, Kenneth R. French, Ph.D., Data Library, Standard and Poor's, Yahoo! Finance, Russell Investment Group, and the Federal Reserve Bank of St. Louis. Where available, dividend adjusted data are used to calculate historical performance returns. Calculations in the text are based on historical data series available as of September 2007. Actual live signals issued from *ChannelCapitalResearch.com* were used for 2006.

Nothing in this book should be considered as personalized investment advice.

This work is based on publicly available information and what we have learned as financial journalists. The model results described in this book are purely hypothetical and thus have inherent limitations. They may contain errors and you should not make any investment decision based solely on what you read here. It is your money and your responsibility. Furthermore, we do not warrant or represent that the information contained in this book is correct, complete, accurate, or timely. Investments of the type discussed in the book may involve appreciable risks, including the risk that most or all of the investor's principal may be lost. We will not be responsible for any investment decisions, damages, or other losses resulting from or related to use of the information we provide.

No representation is made that any account will or is likely to achieve profits or losses similar to those shown, and there are frequently significant differences between hypothetical performance results and those subsequently achieved by following a particular strategy, which can adversely affect trading results. Unlike an actual performance record, simulated results do not represent actual trading. Also, since trades have not actually been executed, the results may not have compensated for the impact, if any, of certain market factors, such as lack of liquidity. Simulated investment programs in general are also subject to the fact that they are designed with the benefit of hindsight. This cannot be fully accounted for in the preparation of model performance results. As with all historical data, past performance is not a guarantee of future results. All investments involve risk, including loss of principal.

*To Nancy, Elizabeth, and Alexander
for all your support
and
To the readers with the courage to stand
apart from the crowd and chart their own
path to investment success*

Contents

Foreword

I'm not easily impressed. I've been in the world of finance and investment long enough to have developed a keen sense of who is for real and who is just putting on a good show. I tell you this because it is important for you to understand that I don't say things like this gratuitously—Doug Roberts is one of the smartest people I've ever met, and is a visionary when it comes to investing. I have known Doug since high school and have been in touch with him on and off through the years. Although our paths did not cross as often as I would have hoped, I made it a point to keep abreast of his research and developments in his strategies. His work has always been highly regarded by investment professionals although, as you will read in this book, many of them wish he was in another line of work.

Doug is correct when he says that most investment professionals do not outperform the S&P 500 over time—I consider myself one of the rare exceptions—so I was intrigued when I first read Doug's research on the Federal Reserve and how it correlates with stock market performance. I wish I could tell you that I was surprised but, as I said earlier, I am fully aware of his capacity to come up with amazing ideas. The testing of his research was done with great care, and, in my opinion, he has made every effort to find errors or flaws in his work. But facts are facts, numbers don't lie, and Doug's Follow the Fed® investment strategies make sense for the vast majority of people.

Follow the Fed is great for those who don't want to make growing their wealth into another career. It is easy, inexpensive and, over time, should make you a lot of money. That said, understanding the concepts in this book will also be of great value to the more active investor. No matter what your investment strategy may be, Follow the Fed offers crucial insights into factors that can guide you in your own strategy. I can attest to that, as I have used Doug's research in many of my own decisions.

HILARY KRAMER
AOL Finance Editor
New York City

Preface

As anyone interested in the subject of profitable investing knows, there's a wealth of books currently available on
the subject. Why, you ask, should you read this book—as
opposed to any of the others out there?

*Follow the Fed to Investment Success: The Effortless Strategy for
Beating Wall Street* is a landmark in the field. Where others
advise you how to become a superior stock analyst, building
a portfolio rich with valued stocks, and then watching the
market like a hawk, I offer you a simpler, less-exhausting way
to be a more successful investor.

This book is intended for people just like you. Perhaps
you're new to investing. Perhaps you've tried your hand at
stockpicking and lost money, worried yourself sick about the
state of the market, and spent far too much precious time
in relation to the meager gains made by your portfolio. You
are looking for an easier way, a more intelligent way, to build
your assets through investing. In other words, *Follow the Fed
to Investment Success: The Effortless Strategy for Beating Wall Street*
is for anyone with some time, some investable money—but
with no desire to be consumed by stock watching and market analysis.

What you hold in your hands is just the beginning. As
you read through the chapters, you'll be invited to use the
resources made available on my companion Web site, www.
FollowtheFedtheBook.com. These include additional readings for the extremely curious, but more importantly, they
include the worksheets and resources I have created for each
of the later chapters. Each will guide you through the process of applying the principles of the Follow the Fed Standard Strategy to build your investment portfolio. The goal of

this two-pronged approach is simple: to provide you with the information you need and to assist you in the practical application of that information.

The book consists of 14 chapters, followed by an Appendix, Glossary, and Notes. The first four chapters detail my own experiences with Wall Street, in addition to a historical look at the evolution of the market and the investing mindset that exists today.

Chapter 1. Where Are the Customers' Yachts? A Typical Investor's Experience with Wall Street

This chapter tells the story of a typical investor and his experiences with Wall Street. It also reviews the data showing that most brokers and mutual funds do not outperform the S&P 500 with their stockpicking abilities and succeed only in enriching the investment companies that create and sell them.

Chapter 2. A Wall Street Insider's Story: My Search for True Investment Outperformance

This chapter relates lessons I learned during my time on Wall Street that allowed me to take control of my investments and my financial future.

Chapter 3. What the Robber Barons Can Teach Us

Throughout history, success in the stock market has been determined by the actions of the major banks, initially by those owned by the robber barons such as J. P. Morgan.

Chapter 4. The U.S. Federal Reserve—The Robber Baron of Modern Times

This chapter describes how the Federal Reserve was developed to replace the robber barons as the financial powerhouse of the modern world. The second section gets to the heart of things, detailing the Follow the Fed investment philosophy.

Chapter 5. The Edge: Don't Bet Against the House

As the casinos make a fortune by taking advantage of the odds being slightly in their favor, this chapter illustrates the huge effect of slight increases in the return on investment when compounded over long periods of time and demonstrates the tremendous benefits that can be achieved in building wealth with an investing strategy that outperforms the market.

Chapter 6. The Ten Essentials (Plus a Bonus): Requirements for Success with Follow the Fed

This follows the development of the Follow the Fed strategy and reviews the basic requirements that I feel are necessary for the average investor to succeed.

Within these first six chapters I present a total of 22 investment lessons, each with an essential insight or protocol for you to incorporate into your investing mindset. These will be reviewed in the final chapter.

Chapters 7 through 10 concern the analysis of small stocks' performance and document my theory of small stocks' gains and losses.

Chapter 7. The Secret to Beating the Market: Small Stocks

A review of the data that backs up the "small stocks effect," which demonstrates that Small Stocks outperform large stocks as represented by the S&P 500 over an extended period of time. This outperformance can have a substantial effect on building wealth.

Chapter 8. The Catch with Small Stocks

This chapter explains the difficulty of investing in a pure small stocks portfolio for several reasons.

- ◆ Devastating drawdowns in some bear markets
- ◆ Increased volatility
- ◆ Unfamiliarity with small companies
- ◆ Outperformance concentration in short periods

Chapter 9. The Big Question: Why Do Small Stocks Outperform?

This chapter presents my theory that, based on research and analysis. as well as upon my actual experience on

Wall Street and running a small corporation, small companies outperform when money and credit is easily available.

Chapter 10. Proving the Follow the Fed Formula for Small Stocks

This chapter demonstrates my theory that small stocks' outperformance is concentrated during times when money and credit is loose and shows the incredible results.

Chapter 11. Follow the Fed: The Easy Strategy for True Wealth™ Step-By-Step Instructions: Implementing the Standard Strategy in Your Own Portfolio

This is a step-by step procedure for implementing the Follow the Fed Standard Strategy in your own portfolio.

Chapter 12. How to Use Follow the Fed for All types of Investments

This chapter shows how you can use the Follow the Fed® strategy with 401(k) plans, IRAs, Retirement Plans and your Broker or Financial Advisor.

Chapter 13. Advanced Follow the Fed Strategies

Advanced Follow the Fed strategies increase the performance advantage even more than the Standard Strategy.

Many of the chapters include boxed information, each of which provides background or examples, or are otherwise supportive of the chapter text.

Chapter 14 is a review of the 22 Investment Lessons garnered from personal experience and my in-depth research into the history and operation of Wall Street during the past century.

This is where the supporting materials found on the Web site, www.FollowtheFedtheBook.com, will prove to be extremely valuable. I strongly suggest you make use of them to more easily apply the Follow the Fed strategies detailed in this book.

The Glossary and Appendix are supporting materials. Whereas the Glossary is for everyone who has a question about the use of a term within the text, the Appendix was written for those of you who wish to know more about the operations of the Federal Reserve System, the fundamental element of the Follow the Fed strategies.

I would like you to begin with the Introduction, where you will read about my intentions and profound desire for you to profit from learning and applying the Follow the Fed strategy to your own investment portfolio.

Acknowledgments

Although I take credit for authorship, this book would not have been possible without the help and guidance of many people.

I want to thank Jack Bogle, former chairman of Vanguard Funds, for inspiring me through the revolution in low-cost index funds that he started when I was still in business school. I also want to thank Dr. Jeremy Siegel of the Wharton School at the University of Pennsylvania for his contribution and inspiration. It was as a student in his finance class that my initial interest in the investment world was first awakened. I also want to thank Professor Kenneth R. French of Dartmouth College and Standard and Poor's for their contributions.

I am simply adding to the base of knowledge generously built for me by these individuals, along with many others from whom I have learned during my career in investment finance.

I want to thank my own editorial team, which generously gave their time and effort to help create this book: Jeff Schwartz, Dr. Marlene Hollick, Kim Stacey, Aly Hagen, Joe Clancy, Mark Tedrow, Matt Cain, and Anora Mahmudova. I want to extend my deepest appreciation to my talented editors at John Wiley & Sons, David Pugh and Emilie Herman, along with Stacey Small and Michelle Fitzgerald. And what can I say about my amazing literary agent, Maura Teitelbaum, who actually gives agents a good name.

I want to thank my family as well, especially my wife, Nancy, for helping me during the entire process of writing the book, as well as through our unique journey through life. I appreciate the understanding and love of my children, Elizabeth and Alexander. You both inspire me every day of my life. I also want to thank my mother, Flori Roberts, for her insightful comments on the book and my late father, Craig Roberts, for training me to analyze situations without emotion, based purely upon the facts.

Finally, I want to thank and to acknowledge the many others who contributed: Howard Gitten, Esq.; Robert Picard of Optima Fund Management; Jamie Price of UBS Securities; Lew Eisenberg; Andy Melnick, Bob Bly, Joe Sugarman, Mark Blumenkrantz, Henry Fernandez of MSCI; Sam Navarro of Cowen and Co.; Paul Guidone; David Feldman, Esq.; Dave Gagner; Danon Robinson of Toro Trading; Geoff Garbacz of Quantitative Partners; Ron Drazin, Esq.; Sanjay Verma of Morgan Stanley; Monica Logani, Jeff Sutterfield, Ian Heller, Ivo Kurvits, Jef Keep, and Hilary Kramer, Finance Editor of AOL.

Introduction

This book is *not* aimed at aggressive investors such as day traders. It is *not* meant for the person who sits at a computer screen all day worrying about his or her portfolio. It *is* for the person who is tired of being scared by what he hears in the financial news every day. It *is* for the person who wants a great return but is not comfortable with taking huge risks with his life savings. And, finally, it *is* for the person who wonders why his broker is driving a Porsche and he's not!

I write this book for investors who will make the following commitments:

- I will think outside the box and rely on my own common sense.
- I will take charge of my own financial future.
- I will take action to make things happen.

After reading this book, you should no longer have to be stressed by nagging doubts, such as:

- Will I always have to work to live the way I like?
- Can I really lose all the money I invested?
- Will I miss that investment opportunity of a lifetime?
- How can I survive another killer bear market?
- Does successful investing always have to be a second job?

I have something important to tell you about. It's called *Follow the Fed®*, and it will change the way you think about your money and your future. In order for you to really grasp the enormity of this, you need to do something that most of us find incredibly hard—you need to let your guard down for just a few moments. You must suspend your natural skepticism and, just this once, accept that something that looks "too good" may in fact be true.

It was hard for me to believe what I discovered until I spent several years, countless resources, and my own money to prove it to myself. Just let the facts speak for themselves. That is all I ask.

> The way to create real wealth and invest for your future with minimal risk of losing your capital involves the least amount of work.

Let me repeat that. The investment strategy that has beaten the S&P 500 and most mutual funds for the past 79 *years* in testing requires only one or two trades every *two years* and does not rely on risky ventures or paying high fees to brokers. As a matter of fact, it can be accomplished using low-cost index mutual funds.

The conventional wisdom you have been taught by Wall Street about the importance of *stockpicking* is designed to keep you dependent on the investment community with its expensive fees and commissions. When Jack Bogle of Vanguard Funds first introduced low-cost index mutual funds more than 30 years ago and claimed that they would outperform most mutual funds at a substantially lower cost, he was met with similar disbelief and criticism about being too good to be true. However, his original claims have withstood the test of time.

My background is that of a Wall Street insider. I attended the Wharton School of Business at the University of Pennsylvania and received both a Bachelor of Science (BS) and Master of Business Administration (MBA). Upon graduation, I worked as an investment banker with Morgan

Stanley in its offices in New York and London. This gave me an opportunity to observe the workings of Wall Street from the inside.

As I worked on Wall Street, I began to notice a few things.

Investment banking and research is a business, and like any other business, its primary purpose is to generate a profit for its owners. It is not a profession like medicine—there is no Hippocratic Oath in finance. Although many investment bankers and other investment professionals sincerely want their clients to prosper, they will do so only if *they* can make money in the process.

Some of the most successful businesspeople and investors that I saw came from outside the Wall Street community. Warren Buffett is the perfect example. Although he worked in New York and apprenticed with the great Benjamin Graham, the father of value investing, he built his fortune from Omaha, hardly a financial center of the universe. These people utilized investment professionals but were clearly in charge of their own money. They were not intimidated or unduly influenced by these advisors. Many of these individuals did not have the educational pedigree of brokers and bankers like me. Some of my colleagues used to joke about this lack of education and sophistication. However, it did not change the fact that these *outsiders* had the real money and that we were working for them!

I noticed that unorthodox thinking, "outside the box" as it is frequently called, often led to greater success, while conventional wisdom led to conventional results. All the people whom I admired thought for themselves, even if this was initially greeted with skepticism.

Therefore, when I had the chance to leave Wall Street to grow my family's business, I decided to do so. After careful examination of the situation, I felt the opportunity for growth was too great to ignore, although I received quite a bit of grief from my former colleagues about abandoning a promising financial career for the cosmetics business. Regardless, I decided to trust my own instincts. It proved to be the correct path for me. We were able to grow the business quite successfully, and sold it to a multinational pharmaceutical company, then listed on the American Stock Exchange, for over $22 million.

I now had the opportunity to put my money where my mouth was. I am a historian by nature, especially when it comes to the U.S. economy and global economics. I studied the trail of wealth in this country from the robber barons of the nineteenth century to their counterparts in the twenty-first century. I ate up every bit of information available about the economy from the Crash of 1929 to the boom of the 1990s and everything in between. I devoured every book, article, pamphlet, and cereal box that had anything to do with this subject. For the next eight years, I tested and tweaked all of my investment theories, using myself as the guinea pig.

As I began my quest to discover how I could build my own personal wealth, I wondered if the wealthy elite I had observed on Wall Street had resources that I could never hope to duplicate. Then, I learned of a group of people from various walks of life who started with modest means but who were able to become multimillionaires with little effort on their part.

These were the Buffett millionaires, people who made incredible amounts of money by investing in Berkshire Hathaway. It made an incredible amount of money for me with surprisingly little effort. I will talk more about this later in the book.

It was as though a light bulb lit up over my head. The answer was to look for opportunities to invest *with* these Wall Street insiders at attractive prices and then stay on for the ride. I looked for similar situations and was quite successful. I thought that I had finally discovered the secret to success.

Then, the technology boom of the late 1990s arrived, and the tactic of investing in value stocks stopped working. It was a new world whose rules I did not understand. I decided to go back to Wall Street to learn more. I took a position at Sanford C. Bernstein, one of the premier investment research and management firms in New York.

During that time, I began to notice the incredible power of the United States Federal Reserve on the availability of money and credit to the financial markets. It seemed as if then–Fed Chairman Alan Greenspan was in the news almost every day. The Fed seemed to be the 800-pound gorilla, influencing all aspects of the stock market. The importance of corporate performance proved to be minor by comparison. Since my firm focused on individual stocks, my colleagues had little interest in my research.

I decided to leave and to focus on developing strategies utilizing the powers of the Fed, and testing them with my own money. Here, my friends, is where my own skepticism disappeared. I soon found that the type of stocks favored by Fed policy were in general the true outperformers in my portfolio. Much to my delight, this accomplishment required extremely little trading. Eventually, I discovered that excessive trading activity on my part actually *reduced* my returns.

I call my strategy Follow the Fed and to this day I continue refining the formula, adding other criteria and benchmarks to increase the Follow the Fed® comparative advantage even more.

I developed a filter to reduce the number of trades in my Standard Strategy, resulting in the Filtered Strategy. I added other proprietary criteria and was able to increase performance even more with my Proprietary Strategy. What all of these strategies have in common is that they are based on monitoring the Fed and its effect on monetary and credit policy.

May this book be the first step in your new investing life—one of freedom, independence, and security.

Douglas S. Roberts
Shrewsbury, New Jersey
July 4, 2007

CHAPTER 1

Where Are the Customers' Yachts?

A TYPICAL INVESTOR'S EXPERIENCE WITH WALL STREET

I borrowed the title of this chapter from a book written by Fred Schwed Jr., a professional trader who lost a bundle of (mostly his own) money in the Crash of 1929. He described his experiences on Wall Street from an insider's point of view in a remarkably humorous fashion.

More than half a century ago, Fred Schwed Jr., who had survived the greatest of all financial market booms and busts, told the story of a tour bus of Nebraska farmers taken to downtown New York. The guide pointed out the major landmarks, including the Stock Exchange, and waved at the docks in the East River. "There," he said, "you see the yachts of the great Wall Street brokers." One of the farmers' children posed an important question: "But where," he asked, "are the customers' yachts?"

Although the book was originally published in 1940, it is as relevant today as it was then. The Internet with broadband access and real-time quotes has replaced the ticker-tape machine, and the laptop computer has replaced the pencil and the ledger book. However, the essence of Wall Street remains the same.

There is an old joke among investment bankers that states, "If you want a friend on Wall Street, buy a dog." I don't think it is quite *that* bad. In the investment business, just like in any business, there are bad *and* good people. However, in the investment arena, seeing people clearly is *essential* to your financial survival.

Because of the demands of work and family and limits on our time, we sometimes depend too heavily on Wall Street professionals to help with our investment nest egg. Whether you work through a broker or advisor or have chosen to do it yourself, you should always be in control and understand what is happening.

If you were buying a home, you would probably use a real estate agent—but you would not buy the home unless it met your needs and desires at the right price. The same is true with your investment portfolio. After all, it is your money!

The Adventures of Joe Investor: A Cautionary Tale

In order to gain an understanding of how Wall Street operates and the dangers of giving up your investor responsibilities, let us look at the fictional journey of a man we shall call Joe Investor. He represents a composite of different investors that I have observed over time. As the TV crime shows say, the events are true but the names have been changed to protect the innocent.

The cast of this little drama includes five major characters, each loosely based on reality:

Joe Investor: the protagonist of the story. Joe is a likable fellow who wants to be among the investing elite.

Emily Advisor: Joe's accountant and financial advisor for many years. She is reliable, conservative, and honest.

Harry Bigbucks: Joe's golf partner. He is an egotistical investor who enjoys bragging about his financial gains.

Wally Broker: a "man with a plan" who graciously allows those in his inner circle to call him *Mr. Broker.* His firm, Wheeler, Dealer, & Company, is where the elite meet to make lots of money.

A. Hedgefund Guru: the keeper of the investment secrets. Silent, powerful, mysterious. This man has made lots of money but no one really knows how.

The Background

Joe Investor had been extremely successful in his chosen profession and was known for his ability and insight. He fancied himself a keen observer of human nature and aimed to be a high achiever in all his endeavors. Joe decided to approach his investments in the same way, aiming for top-notch performance.

He had used his accountant and financial advisor, Emily Advisor, for most of his financial planning. Ms. Advisor's advice was boring because she tended to stick with low-cost mutual funds. However, the arrangement was convenient because Ms. Advisor was quite familiar with Joe's financial situation and was able to do a significant amount of financial planning for relatively low cost.

The Introduction

Our story begins one sunny day, as Joe was playing a round of golf with his buddy, Harry Bigbucks. As they stood together on the green, the topic of investing arose.

Mr. Bigbucks announced that he used the investment firm of Wheeler, Dealer, & Company exclusively. When Joe inquired further, Harry described how all the true players were also clients of the firm and how a new account representative had been making an absolute fortune for him the last several months in technology stocks. Joe listened and then filed the information away, making a mental note to mention this to his accountant, Ms. Advisor, at their next meeting.

As the year progressed, Harry Bigbucks and the other members of their little golf group seemed to be making a killing. It was all Joe heard about at every social event he attended! As he looked at his account statement each month, which was also rising in value but not at the same blistering pace, he began to feel that he was missing a major money-making opportunity.

Joe talked to Harry about his concerns, and he graciously arranged a meeting with his account representative at Wheeler, Dealer, & Company. At the meeting, Joe was introduced to Mr. Wally Broker (known as Mr. Broker to both his friends and clients).

Mr. Broker was everything that Joe imagined a successful investment representative would be, from his crisp, custom-made suit to his corner office with a mahogany desk and an incredible view of the harbor. The photos on his wall showed him with prominent industrialists, sports figures, and even a former president. Mr. Broker discussed his relationships with all these people in detail and then handed paperwork to Joe to establish an account to get started.

As he reviewed the paperwork, he noticed that Mr. Broker's fees were significantly larger than Ms. Advisor's. He asked if this also included the financial planning that Ms. Advisor did. Mr. Broker responded—with a tinge of annoyance in his voice—that his sole focus was as an investment specialist, not a financial planner.

Joe knew that Ms. Advisor would not cut the fees for the planning services; therefore, Mr. Broker's fees would be an *additional* cost. However, Joe decided to go ahead, thinking it *always* costs money to play with the big guys.

Over the next several months, it looked like the right decision. Mr. Broker had placed him in some technology mutual funds. These funds had higher fees and expenses than Ms. Advisor's boring funds but were outperforming them by huge amount. As Joe attended local social events, he became even more comfortable as he heard about the profits his other friends were making in these funds.

The Big Opportunity

Later on that year, Mr. Broker called Joe and asked him to come down to Wheeler, Dealer, & Company as quickly as possible to discuss an incredible investment opportunity. When he arrived, Joe also saw Harry Bigbucks in the office. At that moment, Joe truly felt like the major player he had always wanted to be.

Mr. Broker announced that the premier hedge fund that he used for many of his clients was now accepting new money. Joe wasn't quite sure what a hedge fund was but noticed that it took 20 percent of the profits in addition to the normal management fees. He also learned that the minimum investment was quite high.

With that amount of money involved, Joe wanted to speak to the man in charge of the hedge fund. Mr. Broker grumbled that this would be difficult to arrange but that he would try.

The following day, the three of them visited the office of the hedge fund's managing partner, A. Hedgefund Guru, known only as "the Guru" to everyone, including his children. As they crossed the trading floor on the way to meet this man, Joe was impressed by his operation, with an array of televisions tuned into news programs around the world.

Mr. Broker announced that he would ask the questions since the Guru was very busy. In response to a question on the state of the market, the Guru simply pointed his right index finger up. Then, when they asked about technology stocks in particular, the Guru pointed his right index finger even higher.

At that point, the Guru took a phone call, listened for two minutes, and proceeded to smash the handset on his desk. Mr. Broker said that this indicated the meeting was over. Joe was not quite sure what had happened but noticed pictures of the Guru with three former presidents, the current president, royalty from five major countries, and the actress who won the Academy Award last year. The Guru was *definitely* a major player.

Joe talked to his long-time accountant, Ms. Advisor, who adamantly advised against participating. Ms. Advisor informed him that this was a risky proposition since no one had a clue what this hedge fund even *did*.

Her words fell on deaf ears. Mr. Bigbucks had already committed to the deal, and Joe could not bear the thought of hearing "I told you so" over their next round of golf if this thing was successful. Joe decided to ignore his accountant's advice.

The Wind Shifts

For the first few months, the hedge fund investment was *incredibly* profitable. It ended the year with stellar returns, even after the fees. (Mr. Bigbucks had bought a Porsche, separated from Mrs. Bigbucks, and began showing up around town with a much younger girlfriend named Rome Hipstone. Rome was the young, blond wild child of the founder of the Hipstone hotel group.) Six months after Joe's initial investment, quite unexpectedly, the returns of the hedge fund turned negative one month. Joe wasn't too concerned; he figured that nothing went straight up. However, he *did* start to worry after there were two more consecutive down months.

Mr. Broker informed him that the firm used some leverage, which had led to some short-term volatility, but that this was a buying opportunity. Mr. Bigbucks decided to double his initial investment, but Joe had a funny feeling and decided not to increase his. The next month, the hedge fund rebounded, and Joe began to wonder if he had made the right decision.

Then, one day shortly after this dramatic rebound, Joe read in the local newspaper that the hedge fund was closing down.

Apparently, the Guru had made a bad bet in the currency market, suffered a nervous breakdown, and had not left his bed in the last week. Joe called Mr. Broker at Wheeler, Dealer, & Company and learned that the losses in the hedge fund were quite substantial and that he would only get back

60 percent of his original investment. Sadly, Joe had learned the first lesson of investing, one of 22 valuable lessons I will be presenting in the coming chapters. A summary of these lessons is provided in Chapter 14.

Investment Lesson #1: Profitable investing is not like a contagious disease that you catch from being around the right people.

Joe visited Wheeler, Dealer, & Company to see what could be done to salvage the situation. Mr. Broker tersely informed him that there was very little to be done. Joe mentioned that he really did not understand much about the risks involved with the hedge fund. Mr. Broker sympathized but mentioned that all this was clearly discussed in the subscription document that Joe had signed. He had even initialed the sections involved.

Joe also realized that he had incurred substantial investment fees in this money-losing investment, and he suggested that Wheeler, Dealer, & Company refund some of them. Mr. Broker again sympathized but stated that the firm's policy allowed no refunds and mentioned that these losses were still less than those of Mr. Bigbucks. This fact did not greatly improve the situation. (By the way, Mr. Bigbucks had reconciled with his wife after he was forced to sell the Porsche to cover his losses and Rome left him.)

Mr. Broker offered to make it up on the next deal, but this was a small consolation. He then offered to have Joe and his wife as guests on the yacht that he had purchased with the year's bonus. Mr. Broker asked Joe not to mention this to Mr. Bigbucks, as there was no way he could invite the Bigbucks, since Mr. Broker and Rome Hipstone were now a couple. Joe had learned the second lesson of investing:

Investment Lesson #2: What makes Wall Street rich does not necessarily make the customers wealthy.

Figuring Out Where Joe Went Wrong

Joe quickly realized that he had no alternative but to accept the situation, but he remained in a deep depression for several weeks. He finally decided to speak to his old friend and ally, Ms. Advisor, to determine just how he got into this situation and how to avoid doing it again.

Ms. Advisor truly felt sorry for Joe since the two had a close and profitable relationship for many years. She mentioned that Joe did not have a clue as to what either she or Mr. Broker was doing with his investment funds. It was as if Joe really just did not care to take part in the important decisions being made on his behalf. When Joe mentioned that he went with his gut instincts about people, Ms. Advisor countered that Joe did not run the rest of his life or business this way. Although Joe might choose to delegate responsibility, he always clearly understood what was involved in all of his businesses. However, in investing, Joe seemed to rely on luck and instinct instead of his own intelligence. It was then that Joe learned the third lesson of investing:

Investment Lesson #3: When it comes to investing, it is better to be smart than lucky! If you are smart, you make your own luck.

The two then tried to analyze why Joe had been attracted to Mr. Broker and the Guru in the first place. Joe mentioned that their initial returns had been incredible. His friend and golfing buddy, Mr. Bigbucks, as well as all the other members of his golf group, had done extremely well during last year, and Joe felt as if he were missing an incredible opportunity. Ms. Advisor asked if Joe had looked at the long-term performance and some of the long-term risks involved. Looking embarrassed, Joe admitted that he had not done any of this. He had been seduced by the opportunity for easy overnight riches.

Ms. Advisor discussed the financial planning that she had done for Joe's business and personal portfolio. When the two first started working together, they spent a great deal of time analyzing Joe's long-term goals for retirement and for his family. They had carefully analyzed the trade-off between the time needed to achieve financial success and the time he wanted to spend with his family. Joe had indicated that, to him, incredible wealth was not worth it if he could not have a life. They had formulated a long-term investment program that was working according to plan, until this disaster occurred.

Ms. Advisor said that the *long-term performance* of his portfolio is what matters. Investment performance can vary in the short term even if it is successful in the long term. By contrast, Joe's hedge fund investment was the exact opposite. It had been quite profitable during a short time period but was a significant loser in the long term. This realization was to teach Joe the fourth lesson of investing.

Investment Lesson #4: Think long term about both *return* and *risk* when analyzing your investment.

The two then discussed Ms. Advisor's preference for low-cost funds, especially index funds. Joe did not understand why Ms. Advisor preferred these boring investments when so many better opportunities seemed to be out there. Why was Ms. Advisor so skeptical about investment options that could produce higher returns? The information that Ms. Advisor revealed in response to this question was truly shocking.

The sad truth is that most mutual funds do not even beat the market (as represented by the S&P 500) over a long-term period, according to the Bogle Financial Markets Research Center (see the figure on next page).

Joe was in disbelief. This seemed to be directly the opposite of all the conventional wisdom that he had read and heard all his life. He asked about all those advertisements that he had read, showing funds outperforming the S&P 500.

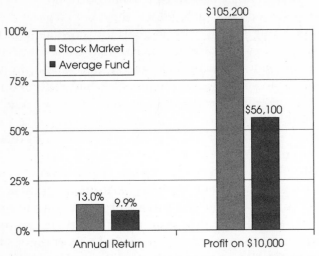

The Stock Market and the Average Equity Fund: 1984–2004

Source: Bogle Financial Markets Research Center, *In Investing, You Get What You Pay For*. Remarks by John C. Bogle, The World Money Show, Orlando, Florida, February 2, 2005. www.vanguard.com

Most Mutual Funds Don't Beat the Market and Can be Hazardous to Your Wealth

Jack Bogle, founder and former chairman of the Vanguard Group, one of the largest mutual fund groups in the United States, argues that most mutual funds do not beat the S&P 500 over an extended period of time. He argues that the stockpicking abilities of most mutual funds do not generate excess returns; instead, they actually cost the average investor money.

Mr. Bogle cites Jack Meyer, former head of the Endowment Fund for Harvard University, who said:

Most people think they can find managers who can outperform, but most people are wrong. I will say 85 percent to 90 percent of money managers fail to match their benchmark. Because managers have fees and incur transaction costs, you know that in the aggregate, they are deleting value. The investment business is a giant scam.

Mr. Bogle also said in a recent speech:

During the period 1984–2004, the average fund lagged the market by 3.1 percentage points per year. While the U.S. stock market, as measured by the Standard & Poor's 500 stock index, provided an annual rate of return of 13.0 percent, the return on the average equity mutual fund was 9.9 percent.

Ms. Advisor replied that many of these advertisements showed the performance over shorter time periods such as 1 or 3 years, rather than longer time periods such as 10 years. Joe said that this sounded quite like the disastrous hedge fund investment that he had just made. Ms. Advisor nodded her head in silent agreement.

Joe asked about the mutual funds that were the true *outperformers* over the long term. Ms. Advisor admitted that there *were* funds like this out there, but there were some additional issues to consider before investing in them:

- Funds like these were quite successful with substantial amounts of money and often were closed to new investors. Joe would not have the opportunity to invest if they are closed to new investors.
- Often, these funds achieved their remarkable track records when they only had a small amount of money under management. They were able to find hidden opportunities that were so small that these were overlooked by the larger investors. Successful track records attract investors' money, and these funds may now be substantially larger than they were previously. With this additional money, they may not be able to achieve the spectacular performance numbers that they achieved before.
- Some of these funds were highly concentrated in a few stocks with minimal diversification. This was fine, as long as the stocks were performing. However, if the

investment manager made a mistake, it could have a disastrous effect on the portfolio.

- The management and other fees for these funds were usually higher than those of the low-cost index funds that Ms. Advisor favored. These fees were usually charged whether or not the funds made money for the investor. Upon hearing this, Joe shuddered in pain, as he recalled the recent conversation on fees with Mr. Broker.

Ms. Advisor agreed that these investment opportunities existed but demonstrated that they were extremely difficult to find. She found it much easier and simpler to focus on consistent, low-cost index funds. With that admission, Joe was to learn the fifth lesson of his investment career.

Investment Lesson #5: Outperforming the benchmark averages, such as the S&P 500, over the long term is much more difficult and rare than is commonly thought.

Realizations and Resolutions

After this conversation, Joe realized how little attention he had been paying to his investment portfolio and how minimal the interest he had shown in its management. This was unusual, since he did not run the rest of his life this way, and the success of his investment portfolio was the key to achieving the lifestyle he had always envisioned. Joe was very fortunate that this last mistake had *delayed* his retirement plans but had not destroyed them.

Joe also realized that he relied too much on other people's expertise. Although Ms. Advisor had been a good choice as a financial advisor, the selection of Mr. Broker had been based on greed and envy.

This was not the only mistake he had made. Joe had not understood what either of these people was doing, and thus had lost control of the situation. Perhaps, if he had discussed this with Ms. Advisor earlier, he might have avoided his hedge fund disaster. He resolved never to let this situation occur again and to have a clear strategy for his investments.

After making this resolution, Joe once again felt in control of his destiny. He began to feel that he could make effective decisions if he used Ms. Advisor or if he did it on his own. He was not going to rely on his emotions or let them run him. Joe realized that taking charge of his investments does not mean taking on another full-time job. He also educated Mrs. Investor, his daughter Princess Investor, and Joe Junior, his son. It was essential that they *all* have the investment tools to prosper in the real world.

Summary

Joe learned many lessons the hard way. His experiences with Mr. Broker and the Guru taught him well. I hope it will teach you, too. Here are the lessons to remember:

Investment Lesson #1: Profitable investing is not like a contagious disease that you catch from being around the right people.

Investment Lesson #2: What makes Wall Street rich does not necessarily make the customers wealthy.

Investment Lesson #3: When it comes to investing, it is better to be smart than lucky! If you are smart, you make your own luck.

Investment Lesson #4: Think long term regarding both *return* and *risk* when analyzing your investments.

Investment Lesson #5: Outperforming the benchmark averages, such as the S&P 500, over the long term is much more difficult and rare than is commonly thought.

The underlying teaching is simple: *Be your own best friend and ally* by learning all you can about investing your hard-earned money. Depending on others is prudent only if they have earned your trust and respect.

For additional information and supplemental resources, visit www.FollowtheFedtheBook.com.

CHAPTER 2

A Wall Street Insider's Story

MY SEARCH FOR TRUE INVESTMENT OUTPERFORMANCE

When you think about investing in the stock market, do you sometimes get the feeling that there are actually two stock markets—one for the average investor and one that favors the Wall Street insider, the true player? These wealthy hedge fund tycoons and corporate investors always appear to have the odds stacked in their favor. Their financial success seems to be easily achieved, as opposed to the struggles experienced by the other 99 percent of the investing population.

I am not talking about moderately wealthy investors. I refer to those who possess billions of dollars in net worth with massive resources at their disposal, and who seem to have the inside track on all the best opportunities. These are the people who are invested in the ventures that deliver the huge paybacks. When I worked on Wall Street, we referred to these opportunities as *tenbaggers*, where your original investment grows tenfold: $10 for every $1 initially invested. You do not need too many of these to accumulate an incredible amount of wealth.

As a young investment banker I was exposed to this unique insider group. Within the Wall Street community *these* people were like an elite club. As a rule, investment professionals tend to be wealthier than their clients; however,

these players were even more successful than the most afflu-
ent investment professionals of Wall Street.

The success of this elite few was in an entirely different
league. They appeared to be gifted with insight and influence that far exceeded the average Wall Street professional.
Many of them achieved success with an unconventional
approach that was initially greeted by the Wall Street community with a great deal of skepticism—and sometimes even
open ridicule.

The Wall Street Elite: An Unconventional Group with Unique Investing Discipline

We have heard a tremendous amount recently about the
private equity firms and their incredible success. However,
when the original private equity groups such as Kohlberg
Kravis Roberts & Co. (KKR) first launched, success was definitely *not* a sure thing.

Long-term success is still elusive for many private equity
firms, but it is worth looking at their completely unorthodox
approach to investing, as it illustrates that thinking *outside
the box* can be exactly the right thing to do. We are going to
examine *leveraged buy-out firms* and *hedge funds*, two innovative,
unconventional investment vehicles of the twentieth century.

Leveraged Buy-Out Firms

A *leveraged buy-out firm* is an entity set up to buy another company using a significant amount of borrowed money (bonds
or loans) to meet the cost of acquisition. Often, these firms
use the assets of the company being acquired as collateral for
the loans, in addition to the assets of the acquiring company.

The purpose of leveraged buy-outs is to allow companies to make large acquisitions without having to commit a
lot of capital. In an LBO, most often the ratio is 70 percent
debt to 30 percent equity, although debt can reach as high
as 90 to 95 percent of the target company's total capitalization.[1] The equity component of the purchase price is typically provided by a pool of private equity capital. Pieces of

the company may be sold to raise additional cash as well. After the debt is reduced to adequate levels, the company is usually either sold or taken public, with the LBO firm reaping a substantial reward.

The idea of using large amounts of debt to acquire a company and then to restructure it and sell it for a huge profit was considered a very risky proposition indeed.

Kohlberg Kravis Roberts & Co.: The Original LBO Firm

When Jerome Kohlberg, Henry Kravis, and George Roberts left Bear Stearns in 1976 to found Kohlberg, Kravis and Roberts (KKR), no one expected them to achieve the level of success and power that they eventually attained. The amount of wealth that they have accumulated far exceeds that of most of their former partners.

Bankers were skeptical that improvements in cash flow could be used to pay down the debts incurred as part of KKR's first deals in 1977: the buy-outs of A.J. Industries, Inc., L.B. Foster Company, and U.S. Natural Resources, Inc. These were not easy transactions; at the time, I heard others on Wall Street say that this would eventually lead to bankruptcy and financial ruin. The naysayers have certainly been proven wrong.

Hedge Funds

The most successful hedge fund firms of today often came from unusual beginnings. It would have been difficult to forecast success when they first started.

The term *hedge fund* dates back to a fund founded by Alfred Winslow Jones in 1949. His strategy was to sell short some stocks while buying others to hold for the long haul, thus hedging some of the market risk.

What is *selling short?* Simply put, selling short is the opposite of going long. When an investor goes long on an investment, it means he or she has bought a stock believing its price will rise in the future. Conversely, when an investor goes short, the anticipation is that the share price will fall. Many investment *pools, syndicates, partnerships,* or *funds* that share characteristics of modern hedge funds were in operation long before Jones set up his hedge fund. However, Jones was one of the first to combine *short selling,* the use of *leverage,* a *limited partnership structure* to avoid regulation, and a *20 percent incentive fee* as compensation for the managing partner. This is why Jones is widely regarded as the father of the modern hedge fund industry.

Stevie Cohen: The Poker Player of the Investing World

Stevie Cohen, the founder of SAC Capital, runs one of the most successful hedge funds in the world. His investing capabilities are in such demand that he is able to charge fees equal to 50 percent of the profits that he generates for his clients and still deliver blockbuster returns. However, despite a degree from my Alma Mater, Wharton, and a brief stint at the firm Spear Leeds and Kellogg, reputedly Cohen's trading skills were acquired as a poker player.

At school, he played in all-night poker games and earned substantial winnings. In these games, he acquired the ability to make quick decisions based on limited information and to assess risk almost instantaneously. He has used these skills to build an incredible fortune.

There is a unique form of hedge fund, one run by a quantitative analyst, not an investment broker. In such funds, the managers build computer-based models to determine whether or not an investment is attractive. In a pure *quant shop* the final decision to buy or sell is made by the model. However, there is a middle ground where the fund manager will use human judgment in addition to a quantitative model.

Although quant hedge funds, as they are called, are quite common today, there was great skepticism earlier. Several firms have been incredibly successful, but not all were. One of the best-known failures was Long-Term Capital Management (LTCM). This firm enjoyed spectacular success until 1998, when its blow-up sent ripples throughout the global financial world. The management of the firm included former senior executives from Wall Street and a Nobel Prize winner.

Jim Simons: The Ultimate "Quant"

Jim Simons is an excellent example of unconventional thinking and the ultimate *quant,* a term used to describe an investor who invests primarily using mathematical strategies. Dr. Simons is a former professor of mathematics at the State University of New York. In 1976, he won the American Mathematics Society's Veblen Prize, one of the world's highest honors in mathematics, for his work in differential geometry.

He has used his mathematical skills at his firm, Renaissance Technologies, to achieve extraordinary investment returns, and has outpaced some of the premier names in the investment world. His firm also employs former academics who have left the world of higher learning for more profitable pastures. These people look for anomalies and inconsistencies in the financial markets that can be used to generate huge profits.

These academics create complex mathematical models to take advantage of the anomalies, with elite Wall Street traders ready to execute their instructions. This unique arrangement has produced returns that are truly astounding.

In some cases, these hedge fund operators have actually experienced a significant failure before finally achieving phenomenal success. This is exemplified by the resignation of Jeffrey Vinik from his management position at Fidelity.

Jeffrey Vinik: Financial Resurrection

When Jeffrey Vinik became manager of the famed Fidelity Magellan Fund, then the premier mutual fund of the world, some said that he had truly reached the pinnacle of his investment career. Magellan was one of the largest mutual funds in existence. Its previous managers included Peter Lynch, who is regarded as one of the legends of the investing world.

When Jeff Vinik made a bad bet in the fund and resigned his position, many assumed that he would never be able to regain such heights. However, the rumors of the death of his investing career were quite premature. He went on to start his own hedge fund and generated much higher returns than when he was at Magellan.

According to the fund's data, Vinik Asset Management returned 440 percent after fees for the four years the fund was in business.

The Boston-based fund was one of the largest hedge funds on the market and has been one of the leading performers in its category. In October 2000, he and his partners chose to close the $4.2 billion hedge fund, citing personal reasons.

People like Simon, Cohen, and Vinik were met with skepticism in their careers. Everywhere they turned, they encountered cynics doubting their abilities and discrediting their achievements.

Value Investors

Warren Buffett is a prime example of a man considered by many investment professionals to be acting irrationally—and succeeding.

Early in his career, Warren Buffett worked on Wall Street and studied finance at Columbia University. His mentor was Benjamin Graham, the man acknowledged in the financial world as the father of *value investing*. Value investing is the strategy of selecting stocks that trade for less than their intrinsic value. Value investors such as Warren Buffett actively seek stocks of companies that they believe the market has undervalued. However, Mr. Buffett surprised Wall Street by returning to his hometown of Omaha, Nebraska, to pursue his unique brand of value investing, initially operating out of his house. The skeptics doubted the wisdom behind such a move—after all, this was hardly a place one would expect to produce one of the richest men in the world.

Lessons from the Elites

We have examined some of the members of this elite club of investors: Jeffrey Vinik, Jim Simons, Steve Cohen, Warren Buffett, and the three founders of KKR.

We did this because common threads run through each of these people. They are *unconventional* investors who are not afraid to think outside the box. But more than that, each has a *disciplined set of rules and methods* that he understands. Lastly, each has enough *confidence* to put his strategies to work without relying on others' opinions.

This leads me to my sixth and seventh lessons on investing:

Investment Lesson #6: To be a successful investor, you have to understand your strategy, to have complete confidence in it, and to take responsibility for your investing decisions.

Investment Lesson #7: A successful investing strategy may be unconventional, controversial, and unpopular.

All of these individuals clearly possessed these characteristics. As a young man embarking on my financial career, I made a conscious decision to try to emulate them.

The Biggest Financial Decision in My Life

When I was working in corporate finance in the London office of Morgan Stanley, a unique opportunity came up—running my family's cosmetics and beauty business in the United States. It was an extremely difficult decision to make. I was one of the youngest associates in investment banking and, at the time, Morgan Stanley was considered the premier firm on Wall Street. I had a solid career path in front of me, possibly leading to a partnership in the not-too-distant future.

Nevertheless, I took the leap and left the firm to work in New Jersey for the family business. I consider it the biggest financial decision of my life. Many of my associates on Wall Street thought that I had lost my mind to give up such a promising career for such a speculative venture. I have to admit—I had my own doubts.

However, it turned out to be the right decision for me. We were able to grow the company through internal means (without acquisitions) from under $5 million in sales to over $20 million in seven years, with an even bigger increase in net profits. In 1992, we sold the entire enterprise to an international pharmaceutical group for more than $22 million.

If I had listened to what everyone was telling me to do instead of relying on my own instincts and analytical abilities, I might have passed up this incredible opportunity. Many of these naysayers were smarter and more experienced than I was. However, this was still the right opportunity for me, and I acted on intuition. In the end, I had demonstrated to myself and others that unconventional thinking can lead to exceptional returns.

The Incredible Revelation of the Buffett Millionaires

Throughout my business career, I have often felt the need to control every situation. Even after delegating tasks, I had to have the final word. With the profitable sale of the business that we built, this seemed like a solid formula. It was typical of other successful businessmen I had observed.

When I started investing, such an approach put severe limitations on my ability to participate in certain business opportunities. Then, I heard about the *Buffett millionaires*, and they literally changed my life by changing my view on investing.

The Buffett millionaires were the people who had invested modest amounts of money in Berkshire Hathaway when Warren Buffett assumed control in the 1960s. People who invested as little as $5,000 became millionaires if they held onto the stock long enough. This was a complete revelation to me! These individuals literally let Warren Buffett do the work and reaped tremendous financial benefits.

I had known about the legend of the "Sage of Omaha," Warren Buffett, but always assumed that I could never make money with him. I assumed that was reserved for the tycoons of finance and industry. However, when I read about the "Buffett millionaires," I started to wonder if there was a way for me to get a piece of this action.

The opportunity came when the stock price of Warren Buffett's main investment vehicle, Berkshire Hathaway, was selling for close to book value, a level that I considered to be cheap. If you're unfamiliar with the term, *book value* is the net asset value of a company, calculated by total assets minus liabilities. I had just received a nice windfall from the sale of our business, so I decided to take a calculated risk. I started buying Berkshire at the end of 1992 and accumulated a position that was a huge portion of my personal net worth at the time.

Many people, including some members of my family, thought I was crazy. However, I believed in what I was doing and resolved to stand by my decision. In the beginning, it was difficult to stand apart from the crowd, but my investment in Berkshire made me incredible returns without any real effort on my part.

The truly amazing thing was that this investment made me much more money than other ventures that would have involved much more work. At first, I could not understand this. However, as I read through all the Berkshire Hathaway annual reports and the investor letters for the original Warren Buffett Investment Partnerships in the 1950s, I realized that he had experienced a similar revelation earlier in his career. He had tried to manage some of the companies in which he invested and realized that this involved a great deal of time and effort and that he was not particularly well-suited to the task. He found that a passive investment strategy was much more successful for him and involved much less work.

This leads to my eighth and ninth lessons on investing:

Investment Lesson #8: Successful investing involves making smart decisions and not necessarily working hard.

Investment Lesson #9: Do not let your ego prevent you from taking advantage of incredible investment opportunities.

The Tech Boom of the Late 1990s: A Turning Point in My Investment Career

With this new insight, I found success with other companies similar to Berkshire Hathaway. These investments were incredibly profitable, often beyond my wildest dreams. The best thing about them was how very little work was required on my part. As long as I had bought the stock at the right price, all that was required was the fortitude to hold it through its fluctuations over time.

However, as the price of Berkshire Hathaway and the stock market in general rose over time, opportunities such as these became fewer and fewer. Value investing no longer seemed to be working. The technology boom had arrived, and it was a phenomenon that did not fit my frame of reference.

I decided to return to Wall Street to try to gain additional insight into this seemingly irrational bull market. I took a position at Sanford C. Bernstein, a Wall Street firm that I felt had the best reputation in investment research and management. I thought that the resources available would help me to understand what was occurring in the rapidly changing investment world.

I learned a tremendous amount about how the invest-ment management side of Wall Street worked. However, the biggest lesson came in discovering that the premier value investors seemed to have no greater understanding of what was happening than I did.

I decided to conduct my own original research. I would utilize other people's insights, but the ultimate responsibil-ity for my investment portfolio was mine. I decided to look at the history of investing, since the past often gives us incred-ible insight into the future. In the next chapter we will do exactly that—step back in time to learn from history.

Summary

In this chapter I shared with you my experiences and the insights gained in my search for true investment outper-formance. Along the way, I learned four more powerful les-sons for investment success.

Investment Lesson #6: To be a successful investor, you have to have complete confidence in your strategy and take responsibility for your investing decisions.

Investment Lesson #7: A successful investing strategy may be unconventional, controversial, and unpopular.

Investment Lesson #8: Successful investing involves mak-ing smart decisions and not necessarily working hard.

Investment Lesson #9: Do not let your ego prevent you from taking advantage of incredible investment opportunities.

More lessons will come from my continued research into past Wall Street performance, and the examination of the strategies, gains, or losses of the major players. This research is the focus of the upcoming chapters.

For additional resources, including my current insights on the market, visit www.FollowtheFedtheBook.com.

3

What the Robber Barons Can Teach Us

It is often said that the answers to the future lie in the past. This definitely proved to be the case for me, and I know it will for you, too. That is why I am taking you on a journey of discovery, the same journey I undertook years ago. We start at the point closest to us today and slowly walk back into time.

The Late 1990s: Valuations No Longer Matter

The late 1990s were a unique time in my investment career. Corporate valuations no longer seemed to matter. Everyone seemed to be focused on owning large-cap growth companies, particularly in the technology area. Traditional measures such as price/earnings, price/book, and price/sales no longer seemed relevant. New valuation parameters such as price/mindshare were devised to justify these valuations. How does one measure *mindshare*? I never did figure that one out.

The new "valuations" appeared to be merely excuses for investors to buy stocks that were rising. All Wall Street needed was some logical justification to recommend these stocks, despite the absurdity of the underlying growth assumptions. However, small-cap value stocks could not get any attention, no matter how attractive the valuations. Since my focus was on value, this was particularly painful on a personal financial level.

It looked to me like a train wreck waiting to happen, so in 1998 I decided to step aside and try to avoid these growth stocks. But then, the large growth stocks rose even more! Some value investors, like Julian Robertson, had shorted these stocks, and they got killed in the short term. Eventually, however, they were proven right. After the bear market of the early 2000s, if they had the fortitude and financial backing to maintain their positions, they were eventually rewarded. Basically, Robertson was out of sync with the timing, and most investors could not stick with him.

Bears and Bulls: Images of Gains and Losses

By definition, a *bear market* is when the stock market falls for a prolonged period of time, usually by 20 percent or more. This sharp decline in stock prices is normally due to a decrease in corporate profits, or a correction of earlier overvaluation.

Investors who are scared by these lower earnings or lofty valuations sell their stocks, causing prices to drop even further. This causes other investors to worry about losing the money they have invested, so they sell as well—and so the fall continues.

One of the best examples of such an unfriendly market was in the 1970s during and after the oil crisis. Stocks stalled for well over a decade, keeping the bear market alive because there were more sellers than buyers.

The opposite, a *bull market*, occurs when almost all stock prices are on the *rise*. A bull market is a prolonged period in which investment prices rise faster than their historical average. Bull markets can happen as a result of an economic recovery, an economic boom, or investor psychology. The bull market of the early 1990s is the longest and most famous in history, during which the U.S. equity markets grew at their fastest pace ever.

This was a painful time for value investors. They were called *dinosaurs*, no longer considered relevant in a new growth era. Like others, I tried to adapt my own strategy to the current situation by arguing (albeit unsuccessfully) that a stock was a value stock simply because it was cheaper than a comparable growth stock. In reality, the stocks I chose were simply less overvalued than others.

Microsoft in the Late 1990s

Microsoft was the Goliath in the stock market of the 1990s. It had grown from a small software partner of IBM to a corporation far larger than it, in terms of market capitalization, in less than 20 years.

Microsoft's operating system software dominated the market for personal computer applications, and its office software dominated the market for word-processing and office-related functions. It had also successfully defeated Netscape for dominance of the Internet browser market.

Microsoft was viewed as a stock that would dominate the market for the foreseeable future. However, it was also incredibly expensive compared to its past history.

Microsoft (June 30, 1999)

Price	$90.19
Basic earnings per share (EPS)	$1.54
Weighted average shares outstanding	5,028 million
Revenue	$19,747 million
Revenue per share	$3.93
Shareholder equity/Book value	$28,438 million
Book value per share	$5.66
Price/Earnings ratio	58.56
Price/Sales ratio	22.96
Price/Book ratio	15.95

Source: Price from www.Yahoo.com. Other data from Microsoft 1999 Annual Report.

My Saving Grace and My Fatal Flaw:
The Need to Understand

Like most investors in the 1990s I made a lot of money and ended up giving much of it back. However, I consider myself lucky because my portfolio never got truly decimated. Other investors were not as lucky. (I based my Joe Investor character in Chapter 1 on a composite of the unfortunate investors I encountered during that time.)

I always need to understand what I am doing when it comes to investments and, honestly, in most other things in my life as well. In my youth, I was the kid who always took the appliances apart to see how they worked. Putting them back together so they operated properly was more difficult, much to my parents' chagrin.

I always viewed investing in technology and growth stocks like a science experiment and used only a small portion of my portfolio. My need to understand this experiment was my flaw, limiting my returns during the boom period, but it became my saving grace during the subsequent tech bust. Although there were people who made money and were able to keep most of it, far more investors—especially ordinary investors—lost money during this period.

This leads to my tenth lesson on investing:

Investment Lesson #10: Investing is like driving a car. Never do it with your eyes closed!

The Go-Go Era of the Late 1960s and Early 1970s

History does repeat itself. I decided to look at similar equity bubble periods in history in order to gain insight into the current situation. My Wall Street mentors always told me about the Go-Go Era of the late 1960s and early 1970s. It had some similarities to the late 1990s—everyone was focused on growth.

It was also considered to be a new era, during which the bulls dismissed previous valuations. There was a joke going around at the time that if you added the suffix -*tronics* to the end of a company's name, it was good for a 20 percent increase in value, since electronics stocks were then all the rage. This sounded very similar to the dot-com phenomenon of the 1990s, when companies such as Globe.com went public, with no perceptible earnings, forming one of the greatest bubbles in the history of finance.

The Foundation of the Go-Go Era: The Nifty Fifty

The *Nifty Fifty* was an informal term used to refer to 50 popular large-cap stocks on the New York Stock Exchange in the 1960s and 1970s that were widely regarded as solid *buy-and-hold* growth stocks. These fifty are credited with propelling the bull market of the early 1970s. Most are still solid performers, although a few are now defunct or otherwise worthless.

The stocks were often described as *one-decision*, as they were viewed as extremely stable, even over long periods of time. The most common characteristics by the constituents were solid earnings growth and a high price/earnings ratio.

Some of the *Nifty Fifty* stocks of the Go-Go Era you'll recognize today:

American Express
Anheuser-Busch
Avon Products
Black & Decker
Bristol-Myers
Chesebrough-Ponds
The Coca-Cola Company
Dow Chemical
Eastman Kodak
Eli Lilly and Company
General Electric
Gillette
Halliburton
IBM
International Telephone and Telegraph
J.C. Penney
Johnson & Johnson

McDonald's
Merck & Co.
PepsiCo
Pfizer
Philip Morris Cos.
Polaroid
Procter & Gamble
Revlon
Joe Schlitz Brewing
Sears, Roebuck and Company
Simplicity Patterns
Squibb
S.S. Kresge
Texas Instruments
Upjohn
The Walt Disney Company
Xerox

This era ended with the 1973 to 1974 bear market and could have been used to predict accurately the tech bust of the 2001. However, this did not offer much insight as to why the phenomenon occurred and why it continued for so long before imploding.

Investing Lessons from Nineteenth- and Twentieth-Century Robber Barons

The growth of the Internet was similar to that of the rise of the automobile in the Roaring 1920s and that of railroads in the late 1800s; so I decided to expand my research even further back into history. Several of my Wall Street colleagues were quite shocked that I was extending my research into what they termed "ancient history" and subtly suggested that I confine my analysis to more recent periods.

However, as I read further, I found that these periods and their economic environments were very similar to the situation in the late 1990s, with one interesting difference. The individuals at the forefront of these periods were able to make even more money than the tech billionaires of the 1990s and seemed to retain more of those gains.

Many derisively called them *robber barons* because their net worth and lifestyle were so far above that of ordinary people. When the stock markets crashed, these individuals did not seem to be affected; they often profited from the downturn. Some believed that their gains were not legitimate and were "robbed" from ordinary people. In some cases, these suspicions were quite correct.

These great robber barons had lavish lifestyles. They owned mansions in places like Newport, Rhode Island, and Palm Beach, Florida. They threw incredible parties and spent their time socializing with royalty, presidents, and heads of state. They were the subject of novels such as *The Great Gatsby* by F. Scott Fitzgerald.

Many of these robber barons did not seem to work particularly hard, either. It was not unusual for them to travel around the world in private yachts that were comparable to an ocean liner. They appeared to be totally in control and able to repeat their success again and again.

The big question was, "How did they do it?" Was it dumb luck, or was there a pattern to these great fortunes? I spent countless hours researching, often turning to the books written years ago by the robber barons themselves. Initially, it was discouraging. I could not find anything that was applicable to me. I was on the verge of giving up when suddenly a pattern emerged. Many of these tycoons had huge banking interests. It was this access to capital that allowed them to shape the fortunes of major as well as many minor companies of their time.

The Rothschilds: The Original Central Bank of European Royalty

There were many prominent banking families in Europe during the 1800s, but few had the international scope of the Rothschilds. In the early 1800s, Mayer Amschel Rothschild, a coin dealer to a German prince, sent his five sons abroad to establish a banking dynasty that would dazzle and dominate Europe for generations.

Each of these sons established Rothschild banks in the capitals of Europe: London, Paris, Vienna, Frankfurt, and Naples. As bankers to the governments and royalty of Europe, the Rothschilds got access to valuable information ahead of the crowd that allowed them to make massive fortunes on their investments.[1]

J. P. Morgan: America's Banker

J. P. Morgan was the preeminent banker of the late nineteenth and early twentieth centuries. He arranged financing and helped to create the major industrial companies of his day. It is rumored that Queen Victoria of England, upon meeting him at a party, remarked, "Mr. Morgan, I hear that you are the controlling shareholder of the United States of America." The U.S. stock market seemed to rise and fall based on his lending policies.

Other great banking families also appeared to have similar powers to the Rothschilds and J. P. Morgan. The hedge fund and private equity fund titans of today seem insignificant compared to the influence of these great banking families.

Daniel Drew: The Original American Robber Baron

Daniel Drew may not have been the best-known robber baron of the nineteenth century. However, for a time, he was certainly one of the most ruthless and effective. From a cattle driver with only a minimal education, he became, for a brief period, one of the richest men in America.

He knew the value of money and shorted the stocks of companies that were about to have their credit lines pulled. In one case, he actually shorted the shares of a company in which he was on the board of directors.[2] The ability of companies to grow and to prosper depended on the money and capital that these banking robber barons could provide or deny. Those companies who could obtain loans on favorable terms were able to prosper, usually enriching their shareholders. Many times the shareholders included the bankers who financed them in the first place. Often, other robber barons were able to piggyback on these moves, either informally or as a syndicate designed to manipulate stock prices, enriching everyone involved.

This led me to my eleventh lesson of investing:

Investment Lesson #11: The golden rule of investing history is, "He who hath the gold maketh the rules."

Joe Kennedy: Avoiding Disaster by Staying a Step Ahead of the Market

Ambassador Joseph P. Kennedy, the father of President John F. Kennedy and the creator of the Kennedy family fortune, seemed to have an amazing ability to be in the right place at the right time. However, the most incredible talent the Ambassador possessed was his ability to stay one step ahead of disaster.

Joe Kennedy was a successful banker and speculator in the stock market during the 1920s, but he largely avoided the commonly devastating effects of the Great Depression by pulling most of his money out of the stock market before the Crash of 1929.

As a matter of fact, despite his checkered past (and maybe because of it), Kennedy became the inaugural chairman of the Securities and Exchange Commission (SEC) when it was created by President Franklin Roosevelt in 1934. FDR is said to have explained this choice by saying, "It takes a thief to catch a thief."

Kennedy's financial instincts also led him to one of the few industries that was profitable and growing in the 1930s. He correctly reasoned that alcohol would be one of the few bright spots in the Depression after the repeal of Prohibition, (perhaps because he was trading in it during Prohibition), and during a trip to London with the president's son after the 1932 election, Kennedy was able to successfully secure the sole American distributorships of two premium scotches and Gordon's gin.

Source: Seymour M. Hersh, *The Dark Side of Camelot* (Little, Brown & Company, Boston, 1998), pp. 44–63.

Summary

Of all the interesting characters in America's history none have been more powerful than the robber barons of the nineteenth and twentieth centuries. Studying their achievements and the context in which they were made led me to these two lessons in investing.

> **Investment Lesson #10:** Investing is like driving a car. Never do it with your eyes closed!
>
> **Investment Lesson #11:** The golden rule of investing history is, "He who hath the gold maketh the rules."

The banking reforms of the early twentieth century were designed to eliminate the unfair investing advantage of these robber barons. To a large extent, the government was successful. However, to my surprise and shock, I discovered that the system of preferred lending and financing that enriched those early tycoons remains the same today, only with different players and methods. So, let us move on to review the creation of the Federal Reserve Bank, the entity I consider to be the newest, and most powerful, robber baron.

For additional supportive materials and resources, visit www.FollowtheFedtheBook.com.

4

The U.S. Federal Reserve—The Robber Baron of Modern Times

We are now going to move from those highly successful business entrepreneurs of the late 1800s and early 1900s known as the robber barons, to the rise of an institution that bears many of the same characteristics: the Federal Reserve System. Before we do so, I would like to comment once again on the lifestyle and social position of the prestigious robber barons.

As I mentioned in the previous chapter, the robber barons led very privileged lives, almost like royalty. The power they possessed was incredible, but they also had the enormous responsibility to maintain the stability of the U.S. banking and financial systems, even though such responsibilities were balanced by the incredible opportunities for them to profit from their actions.

The banking reforms of the early twentieth century sharply curtailed the powers of the great U.S. banking institutions to influence the financing and credit policy of the United States. Their financial powers were transferred to a new American central bank, the U.S. Federal Reserve System, also known as the Fed. This created a financial power of immense proportions, dwarfing the power of the robber barons and their banks.

The establishment of the Fed largely eliminated this conflict of interest, since monetary authorities are not dedicated to making a profit but are committed to the welfare of the country as a whole. However, the Fed's banking and monetary policy continues to affect the economy and the stock market on an even more massive scale.

The Origins of U.S. Central Banking

The idea of a U.S. central bank has been a controversial topic throughout American history, inflaming passions and bitter disputes whenever it was discussed and debated. Proponents claimed that it was an absolute necessity in order for the United States to emerge as a major world power and to have a stable currency and banking system. Opponents claimed it was an unfair infringement on states' rights and the free enterprise system and would be exploited to the detriment of the country by powerful, unscrupulous entrepreneurs.

One of the earliest attempts to establish a U.S. central bank was the First Bank of the United States, chartered by Congress on February 25, 1791. The bank was the brainchild of Alexander Hamilton, then Secretary of the Treasury, and was designed to handle the financial needs of the newly formed United States of America. The plan was to create a uniform, centralized financial system instead of the confusion produced by the plethora of state banks, currencies, and economic policies.

Since the northern states were more industrialized and had a well-developed merchant class, they stood to benefit from a strong central bank. The southern states relied primarily on agriculture and distrusted most forms of centralized authority, believing that it impinged on states' rights. This dispute continued with no real resolution until the Civil War. You may think political partisanship is intense in the twenty-first century, but it is absolutely genteel in comparison to the arguments and frequent physical violence that occurred on the floor of the national legislature in the late 1700s and early 1800s.

After all, multiple currencies were in circulation, often issued by such varied institutions as states and cities and even stores and other local businesses. This made conducting ordinary financial transactions exceedingly difficult and chaotic. Remember, there was no central exchange on which you could quickly determine the value of these various currencies. Speculation was rampant, and the daily operation of the central government was problematic.

Alexander Hamilton wanted to model the First Bank of the United States after the Bank of England and to empower it with these primary goals:

- To establish a U.S. Mint with a standard coinage and currency
- To establish an excise tax
- To establish domestic and foreign credit to allow the new nation to borrow more effectively
- To establish financial and monetary policy and order

The bank was established as a private company with a federal charter from 1791 to 1811., It would thereafter be Congress's decision to renew the charter.

The First Bank of the United States continued to encounter opposition from the South, whose political representatives realized the immense potential power of a central bank and feared that this power would be used against the southern economy. Secretary of State and later President Thomas Jefferson, a native of Virginia, was one of the most vocal opponents. Eventually, he and his compatriots prevailed. The First Bank's charter expired in 1811 and was not renewed.

However, this did not eliminate the need for a central bank. The Second Bank of the United States was chartered just four years later, in 1815. President James Madison, originally an opponent of the First Bank of the United States, desperately needed to stabilize the currency and to finance the national debt from the War of 1812. He needed a central bank to accomplish this goal.

The Second Bank's lending policies were controversial. After the War of 1812, the United States experienced an economic boom, due in part to the devastation in Europe from the Napoleonic Wars. Because of the widespread damage to Europe's agricultural sector, the U.S. agricultural sector underwent an expansion. The Second Bank aided this boom through its lending, which encouraged speculation in land.

Essentially, this lending allowed almost anyone to borrow money and to speculate in land, sometimes doubling or even tripling the prices of property. The land sales for 1819 alone totaled some 55 million acres.[1] With such a boom, hardly anyone noticed the widespread fraud occurring at the Bank nor the economic bubble that had been created. After this relatively easy lending policy, the bank instituted a policy of contraction, where loans were called in and credit was no longer available. This tightening may have been the primary cause of the Panic of 1819. The power of an American central bank was substantial even during the early era of U.S. history, and it quite literally determined the economic direction of the country.

The earlier tension between North and South regarding an American central bank continued throughout the existence of the Second Bank of the United States. This animosity came to a climax as the expiration of its charter approached in 1836. President Andrew Jackson from Tennessee thought the Second Bank was corrupt and a threat to society and wished to end the bank's tenure as quickly as possible. Although its charter was bound to run out in 1836, Jackson wanted to put an end to it even earlier. Jackson is considered primarily responsible for its demise, seeing it as an instrument of political corruption and a threat to American liberties.[2]

Senator Daniel Webster of Massachusetts, who was also the Second Bank's legal counsel, took the opposing point of view, calling the Jackson position a "manifesto of anarchy." However, when President Jackson won reelection in 1832, the Second Bank of the United States charter expired in 1836, and it went bankrupt several years later. That was the end of a central bank in America until the early twentieth century.

The Uneasy Peace between the United States and the Robber Barons in the Late 1800s

The tension between the North and the South over the creation of an American central bank continued up until the 1860s, when the Civil War resolved the conflict. The South withdrew from the Union, thus effectively eliminating the major source of opposition. As in the earlier War of 1812, the United States also needed an effective means of financing the war against the Confederacy.

However, because of the fraud, corruption, and the tremendous financial power associated with the Second Bank of the United States, the concept of a central bank was still incredibly unpopular in some circles. As there were also concerns with the constitutionality of several of the Lincoln administration's war policies and restrictions on civil liberties, starting a new central bank would have added to the controversy.

The solution was the National Banking Act of 1863, creating a system of banks that allowed the country to conduct its business. Since several of the robber barons controlled many of these institutions, this only served to enhance their power with an official seal of government approval.

As part of this arrangement, these national banks were responsible for the stability of the financial system. Although they took this responsibility quite seriously, they were private institutions whose goal was to make a profit. Needless to say, this led to quite a conflict of interest.

As with the earlier case of the Second Bank of the United States and the Panic of 1819, a tightening of credit and issuance of new loans created bank "panics" in 1873, 1893, and 1907. As I mentioned in the previous chapter, these events were often quite profitable for many of the more savvy participants involved. However, they were quite disruptive to the country's economic growth and national health.

After the panic of 1907, Congress decided it could no longer tolerate the status quo and created the National Monetary Commission to devise a plan to reform the banking system. A U.S. central bank was once again politically feasible.

The Birth of the U.S. Federal Reserve

Senator Nelson Aldrich from Rhode Island headed the National Monetary Commission and was initially opposed to a central bank. He eventually changed his mind after analyzing the success of Germany's banking system. In 1910, Senator Aldrich, along with executives representing major banks, including J. P. Morgan and John D. Rockefeller, attended a conference in Jekyll Island, Georgia, to address this issue. At this meeting, Paul Warburg of Kuhn, Loeb & Co. directed the proceedings, and the primary features of the Federal Reserve Act were written.

Initially, Senator Aldrich proposed a private central bank called the National Reserve Association. However, the distrust of a central bank that would be controlled by the wealthy banking establishment for its own personal benefit had not disappeared. Many remembered how the robber barons had used the national banking system to enhance their own power and wealth.

In this case, the battle was not between North and South but instead between East and West. The biggest critic of the plan was Secretary of State William Jennings Bryan from Nebraska. He was a populist, well known for his "Cross of Gold" speech at the 1896 Democratic convention. He greatly feared the influence that the northeastern bankers would have in such a central bank.

Eventually a compromise was reached, and the Federal Reserve was born as a quasi-governmental, quasi-private banking institution in 1913. The Fed consisted of a system of 12 regional banks to dilute the influence of the northeastern banking establishment, although the Federal Reserve Bank of New York was solely responsible for conducting open market operations at the direction of the Federal Open

Market Committee (FOMC). The president would appoint the board of governors, along with its chairman.

Federal Open Market Committee

The FOMC is the branch of the Federal Reserve Board that determines the direction of monetary policy and is composed of the board of governors, which has seven members, and five reserve bank presidents. The president of the Federal Reserve Bank of New York serves continuously, and the presidents of the other reserve banks rotate in their service of one-year terms.

The FOMC meets eight times per year to set interest rates—the key federal funds rate and the discount rate—and to decide whether to increase or to decrease the money supply, which the Fed does through buying and selling government securities. For example, to tighten the money supply or to decrease the amount of money available in the banking system, the Fed sells government securities.

The meetings of the committee, which are held in secret, are always the subject of much speculation on Wall Street.

This difficult birthing process also happened to coincide with the need for financing as World War I began, just as the Second Bank of the United States had started with the need to finance the War of 1812. Politics, war, and money make for strange but entwined bedfellows.

As evidence for this suspicion, I offer the fact that Paul Warburg of Kuhn, Loeb & Co. (who had been highly criticized for his banking connections) was appointed by President Woodrow Wilson as the first chairman of the Federal Reserve. This was a questionable beginning for the most powerful banking institution in the world.

Did the Federal Reserve Cause the Great Depression?   The Federal Reserve concentrated an immense amount of financial power in the hands of a few central bankers, who had limited experience on which to base their decisions. Although the government was in control, this did not guarantee that the Fed's decisions would be the right ones. The Fed had the power of creation and destruction on a scale far exceeding the country's earlier banking experiments, and even that of the most powerful of the bankers of the nineteenth century. The wish for a central banking system to support and to direct the finances of the nation was probably a major cause of the Great Depression—the historical calamity that still affects many people living today.

The late Milton Friedman, the Nobel Prize–winning economist from the University of Chicago and the Hoover Institute, documented that the Fed's response to the Crash of 1929 was largely responsible for the bear market and Depression of the 1930s.

He has an interesting point. Even though the Fed initially loosened monetary policy in response to the Crash of 1929, releasing credit and making money freely available, it soon attempted to prevent speculation by tightening credit. Dr. Friedman believes that the Fed began to tighten too quickly.

According to him, this restriction of credit by the Fed triggered a series of bank failures that became widespread. The domino effect of these closures, the lay-offs, loss of housing, and loss of agricultural output could not be stopped until it had run its course. The end result was the Depression of the 1930s, from which it took years to recover.

In many ways, this was similar to the earlier mistakes of the Second Bank of the United States in the early 1800s. However, the Fed's influence was much more extensive in the U.S. economy, which was by then no longer an agrarian society. Because of the increasing industrialization of the country, the effects of any mistakes were magnified.

The Easy Money and Inflation of the 1970s.   The Fed's easy money policy of the 1970s also had a tremendous effect on the economy. It allowed inflation to spread, eventually resulting in the stagflation of the late 1970s. Basically, *stagflation* is a period of slow economic growth and relatively high unemployment, truly a time of economic stagnation, accompanied by a rise in prices, or inflation.

During the 1970s, the rise in world oil prices created sharp inflation, not just in the United States but in all developed oil-dependent countries. For these countries, including the United States, stagnation increased the inflationary effects.

This period eventually ended with the appointment of Paul Volcker as the chairman of the Federal Reserve Board under President Jimmy Carter. The new chairman announced a policy of targeting money supply aggregates to control inflation. This policy was incredibly successful, with inflation dropping dramatically through the early 1980s.

The 1987 Crash and the Testing of Alan Greenspan.   Alan Greenspan became chairman of the Federal Reserve in mid-1987 and then guided the Fed through its greatest test since the Crash of 1929 and the subsequent Great Depression. In October 1987, the stock market experienced a crash in magnitude and duration very similar to the one that occurred in 1929. Many were predicting that history would repeat itself and a depression or at least a severe recession would follow.

Then, something that very few people expected happened. The stock market, as measured by the S&P 500, recovered and actually finished the year in positive territory, rising with a total return of 5.25 percent. This almost matched the return on Treasury bills. If you had moved your assets into cash at the beginning of 1987, it would have made very little financial difference to you by the end of the year.

Several investors sold their portfolios on the recovery, exiting the market altogether. They chose to hold on to their cash, while watching and waiting for the next big crash. Because they acted on their fear and inherent pessimism, they missed many a golden opportunity as they sat predicting that history would repeat itself in the coming years.

However, the S&P 500 registered positive returns every year until 2000, with the exception of a 3.10 percent decline in 1990. Those who had exited the market missed out on one of the longest bull markets in history.

What was different this time? The answer is the actions of the Federal Reserve. Chairman Greenspan was very quick to inject liquidity in the form of increased availability of credit into the market to deal with the crisis and was very careful in withdrawing it. He had learned from the mistakes of the earlier central bankers and acted very differently.

The difference between the outcome of 1929 and that of 1987 demonstrates the incredible influence of the Federal Reserve. In one case, we experienced the most severe depression in our economic history. In the other, we experienced one of the longest and most powerful bull markets. This financial power of the Fed is unprecedented in terms of global banking history.

You can see the importance of the Fed on your investment portfolio as well. Exiting the market after the partial rebound from the Crash of 1929 would have saved your stock portfolio from the great Depression. However, exiting the market after the rebound in 1987 would have prevented you from capturing the profits from the bull market of the late 1980s and 1990s. In essence, fortunes could have been made by *Following the Fed!*

Summary

As I noted earlier in the chapter, the establishment of the Fed largely eliminated the conflict of interest between banks. However, Fed banking and monetary policy often had adverse effects on the economy and continues to affect the economy and the stock market on a massive scale. The salient points in this discussion are as follows:

- Central banks concentrate an incredible amount of financial and economic power in a single organization.
- The Federal Reserve is perhaps the largest and most powerful central bank in history.

The different outcomes to the Crashes of 1929 and 1987 demonstrate the incredible importance of correctly interpreting the Fed's actions on the economy and one's portfolio.

Visit www.FollowtheFedtheBook.com for resources and up-to-the-minute assessments of market activities.

CHAPTER 5

The Edge™: Don't Bet Against the House

You now know how the robber barons used the banking and monetary system to their advantage to control stock prices and to attain great wealth. However, you are probably wondering how this is going to put *you* on the road to financial freedom and true wealth. I am happy to tell you that, while you obviously do not have the ability to control the banks, you *do* have the ability to watch what they do, anticipate the results, and invest accordingly.

But first, let us talk about what *not* to do.

A Brief Review of Conventional Investing Wisdom

Conventional investing wisdom says that the best way to achieve wealth is to invest in a diversified portfolio of large stocks, often through a well-managed mutual fund, and then to wait. This technique is sometimes called *buy and hold*. If you invest in a mutual fund that tracks the most common large-cap stock index, the S&P 500, you would probably get around a 10 percent annual return on your money.

Over an extended period of time, this can definitely create wealth, as Table 5.1 illustrates.

This is pretty amazing when you consider that someone with as little as $10,000 can become a millionaire over

Table 5.1   The Power of Compounding

Time Period	Value of an Initial $10,000 Investment
5 years	$16,105
10 years	$25,937
25 years	$108,347
35 years	$281,024
50 years	$1,173,909
75 years	$12,718,954

a long enough time. This means that a student who works and saves during high school and puts all his money into this buy-and-hold strategy would be a millionaire by retirement. Alternatively, if you put the money into this strategy upon your children's birth, they can become millionaires by their retirement.

The Problem with Buy and Hold

Before you put all your money into the S&P 500, you may want to consider a couple of things:

- This strategy can be extremely volatile over shorter periods of time, particularly if you start investing at the beginning of a bear market for large stocks. This means enduring an incredible amount of pain and stress until the strategy starts working. Not everyone has the stomach for this.
- Many people do not begin to prepare for their retirement until they reach their 30s. They do not have 50 years to let the strategy work.

One possible solution to this is to put additional funds into your investment program. This is a great idea, which I totally support and encourage. Try to save the maximum amount that you can. However, there are factors that limit the amount by which we can reduce our daily expenses, such as health issues and education for your children.

The Potential Solution: The Edge

If you cannot add additional money to your investment program, then, the conventional wisdom of *buy and hold* may not lead you to the financial independence that you always envisioned. What is the solution?

The solution is The Edge™.

What is The Edge? *The Edge* is a small increase in the return on your investment that allows you to reach your financial goals much faster. We are not talking about a get-rich-quick scheme. We are talking about minor increases in returns that can make big differences in your wealth.

Let me illustrate my point by showing you the value of an initial $10,000 investment at different rates of interest over time (Table 5.2). The interesting thing about this table is the power of time. As the time horizon lengthens, the power of small increases in the rate of return is incredible! This is why Einstein once referred to the power of compound interest as "the eighth wonder of the world."

In order for The Edge to work, you have to have a longer time horizon. Let us examine a 10 percent and a 20 percent rate of return at 10-year and 25-year time horizons. Using a 10-year time horizon, the difference between the ending values of a $10,000 investment is $25,937 versus $61,917, more than double your money. However, at a 25-year time horizon, the difference is $108,347 versus $953,962, almost ten times your money. This difference increases even more as we lengthen the time horizon further.

Table 5.2   Compounding with Higher Returns

Time Period	10%	13%	16%	20%
5 years	$16,105	$18,424	$21,003	$24,883
10 years	$25,937	$33,946	$44,114	$61,917
25 years	$108,347	$212,305	$408,742	$953,962
35 years	$281,024	$720,685	$1,803,141	$5,906,682
50 years	$1,173,909	$4,507,359	$16,707,038	$91,004,382
75 years	$12,718,954	$95,693,681	$682,887,545	$8,681,473,693

Getting The Edge: A Trip to the Casino

In order to understand the tremendous power of The Edge in equity investing, let us take a visit to a Las Vegas gambling casino. Here we examine the various characters and their counterparts in the investing world.

The Average Player

You know this guy, the one who gets off the bus expecting to make a killing at the casino but has no clue what he is doing. Casino management will pay a premium to get average players into the casino in the form of free drinks, complimentary meals, hotel rooms, and shows because they know it is only a matter of time before they get their money back (and much more). Despite the freebies, this will be an incredibly expensive vacation. Average players often play the games with the worst odds, such as the slot machines.

This is typical of the average participant in the stock market. He has no idea what he is doing. He generally has no strategy and, even if he has a strategy, like buy and hold, he is unable to stick to it. Thus, his return in the long-term does not equal the return of the S&P 500. He is a loser, just like in the casino.

The Gambler

This guy is a smooth operator. He focuses only on games where the odds favoring the house are limited. Gamblers may be card players and often try to change the rules in their favor. Gamblers are disciplined, which is what prevents disaster. Gamblers make a living but never are able to get truly wealthy because it is very difficult to change the odds.

This is the S&P 500 index investor that we discussed earlier. These investors make money and do well if they are truly disciplined and can stay in it for the long term. However, index investors must have nerves of steel.

The Player on a Winning Streak

You have seen this guy before. He is at the craps table with a crowd of new-found friends around him, including the pretty girl throwing the dice for him. He is having the time of his life—the center of attention and the life of the party. Everyone on the casino staff is giving him the deference and courtesy due a high roller. This guy is on top of the world. There is only one problem: Players do not know how to quit while they are ahead. That is why the casino staff treats them so well. They know that if they encourage Players to believe that this is skill, not just luck, they will continue to gamble until eventually they give all the money back. If it does not happen today, it will happen before the end of the trip. Players should not be mistaken for Gamblers. They have no system or discipline.

In the stock market, most traders, especially day traders, fit neatly into this category. There are some who may fit the category of the Gambler, but, in general, they mistake luck for skill. Instead of knowing when to quit, they continue until they lose. If they have backers, they drag them down with them. The odds are stacked against them, something they will eventually find out—the hard way.

The Underworld

The *Underworld* refers to the underground gambling establishments, bookmakers, and other assorted shady characters that inhabit the gambling world outside the legitimate casinos. These individuals already have their hands on your money the day that you start dealing with them. They make many outrageous promises to get you involved because once this happens, they own you.

In the world of investing, these are the get-rich-quick schemes that promise to turn $1,000 into $1,000,000 overnight, not over time. They play on your worst emotion—greed. Sadly, many who buy into this are those who can least afford to lose their money.

The Card Counter

The card counter is the one that the casino truly fears. This person has a system that can turn the odds in his favor. Therefore, given sufficient time, he can beat the house, sometimes for truly large amounts of money. Card counters usually have a mathematical background, an extremely high IQ, and incredible discipline and tenacity. They can make a tremendous amount of money for their backers.

The only problem with card counters is there are very few really good ones. The casino is always trying to shut them down. If it finds out that someone is counting cards, that person is banned from the casino. Thus, card counters employ disguises, deceptions, and other ploys to escape detection. It is a difficult way to make money, the reason why there are so few of them. Several write best-selling books detailing their adventures after being banned from the casinos.

In investing, these are the true Wall Street wizards. These are people like Warren Buffett, Paul Tudor Jones, and a handful of other great legendary traders and investors. There are so few of them because of the skill and temperament required to practice their craft. Many people claim that they belong to this class of investors, but most do not qualify and are merely traders on a winning streak. They eventually reach the end of the line and burn out, taking their partners with them.

The problem with these investors is that when they become large and successful, they find it extremely difficult to practice their craft undetected. The market takes away their edge. If you can find a true investing wizard early in his or her career, you have a good chance to make a great deal of money. The Buffett millionaires are an excellent example. These people were fortunate enough to invest in Berkshire Hathaway, Warren Buffett's investment vehicle, early in his career. By investing small amounts of money, they were able to become multimillionaires over the years.

However, it is not easy finding this rare breed. Even if you do, your timing has to be right. If both of these things fall into place for you, remember not to tell anyone. You do not want to accelerate the process of losing their edge.

The Gaming and Local Authorities

The gaming and local authorities regulate and tax the casino. They take a piece of everything the casino makes in the form of taxes, including their restaurants, hotels, nightclubs, golf, and other recreational activities. They do not really care who wins or loses, since they make money either way. All they want you to do is to keep gambling. They entice you with great slogans, like "What happens in Vegas stays in Vegas." They fail to mention that one of the things that stays in Vegas is your money.

Their counterpart in the investing world is—you guessed it—the Wall Street establishment. These are the majority of brokers, advisors, investment bankers, and other assorted characters. They do not care whether you make money or lose it as long as the fees and commissions continue to roll in to pay the bonuses that finance the Wall Street lifestyle and pay for those huge McMansions in Greenwich or the Hamptons.

Do not get me wrong, I know many investment professionals who do truly have their clients' best interests at heart. However, they are few and far between. If you happen to find one, treat him or her like a valuable treasure.

And Finally, the House

In gambling, the casino is called the House. It sponsors the games and sets the odds. Like any other business, its goal is to make money. How does it do this? By setting the odds in its own favor, naturally. In many cases, the tilt in its favor is not dramatic. It is just enough so that over time it will always make money. If the odds were stacked too heavily in the House's favor, the players might go elsewhere.

Over time, the House will always make money because of these odds, despite the short-term successes of the characters described. The laws of probability guarantee it. Steve Wynn, the impresario who built a huge casino empire after a short but unsuccessful gambling career, once said that the only true way to make it in Vegas is to own the casino.

In the investing world, the banking authority is the House. It sets the odds and determines investing success or failure. In the nineteenth century, it was the robber barons, who always stacked the odds in their favor. In the twentieth century, these immense powers were transferred to the U.S. Federal Reserve and the other central banks. The Fed is truly the House.

Don't Bet Against the House: Get The Edge and Follow the Fed

If you want to be a winner in a gambling casino, the answer is to bet *with* the House, not *against* it, as Steve Wynn suggested. I am not suggesting going out and buying casino stocks. Remember, you may not be getting the same deal as Wynn and the other insiders. However, if you could bet with the House under the same terms as the insiders, *that* would be an extremely attractive proposition, something very few people would refuse.

If you can invest with the odds in your favor like the original robber barons you would have The Edge that we discussed earlier. The incremental higher returns generated by slightly higher odds in your favor would not need to be much to get you to the financial independence and true wealth that you desire (as illustrated in Table 5.2). Following the Fed is the true way to get The Edge you want.

By Following the Fed, time becomes your friend, not your enemy. You have a system that works over time and where the odds are stacked in your favor. Thus, you can afford to wait out those periods where things are going against you because you know that eventually, things will turn around.

For those who try the other paths listed here, such as the Card Counter, I wish you the best of luck. However, remember the sage bit of advice for the novice poker player. If after entering a poker game you cannot figure out who the sucker is, it is probably you.

Do not be the sucker. Get The Edge by following the Fed. It may take longer but it can be well worth it.

Summary

Conventional investing wisdom says that the best way to achieve wealth is to create a diversified portfolio of large stocks, and then hold them long enough to see significant gains. But the buy-and-hold strategy is not always the best one to use. In this chapter I introduced The Edge: achieving your goals with the Follow the Fed strategy. It is not a get-rich-quick scheme, but a long-term strategy of small increases in returns that can make big differences in your wealth.

If you have questions about The Edge, we have answers for you at www.FollowtheFedtheBook.com.

CHAPTER 6

The Ten Essentials
(Plus a Bonus)

REQUIREMENTS FOR SUCCESS WITH
FOLLOW THE FED

The Follow the Fed strategy offers the average investor the opportunity to beat the market by observing the incredible influence of the Federal Reserve on the equity markets. Chapter 4 demonstrated the power that the Fed has on money and credit in the domestic and global economy, and soon I will reveal a practical, proven strategy that average investors can use to tap into this knowledge for their own investment portfolios. It will not require a tremendous amount of work and is easy to implement using low-cost mutual funds.

However, before I go into more detail on the strategy, I want to discuss some requirements that must be fulfilled to achieve success with my Follow the Fed strategy. These are *essential* lessons that I learned during my investment career, where I saw people make the same mistakes repeatedly. Indeed, I made several of these mistakes myself during my own career, often with painful results.

The truly successful investors I observed were the ones who adhered to all these requirements. They were the ones who were in control of their financial destiny.

In some cases, they had billion-dollar portfolios. However, others started with only a small nest egg, which turned into something substantially bigger.

These lessons can succeed with both value and growth investment strategies. I found that when I mastered these concepts, it enhanced both my life and my net worth. I hope that following them will allow you to avoid some of the pain that so many others have experienced.

Remember the Ultimate Goal: Getting Wealthy (or Wealthier)

When choosing an investment strategy that fits your needs, you have to remember that the ultimate goal is to get wealthy or, in some cases, wealthier. True wealth allows us to do the things we want when we want. This can mean different things to different people.

It can mean spending more time with family and friends or being able to travel the world in luxury. It can mean having the option to work when and how you want or the ability to retire from the rat race to a hammock on a tropical beach. You can enjoy your retirement with the security that only wealth can bring.

If you can focus on this ultimate goal, following the other essentials will be much easier. These are the rules that I find must be observed to achieve true wealth. They are not that difficult, but you have to be willing to commit yourself to them. They helped me to achieve my goals, and I believe that they can do the same for you.

The key is focus. In Chapter 2, I discussed two incredibly successful hedge fund managers, Stevie Cohen and Jim Simons. Both have a reputation for laser-like concentration on achieving high returns. This intense focus seems to be a common characteristic of many of the self-made billionaires. This focus on wealth is a trait that will help you deal with the difficulties that you will experience in building a successful investment portfolio.

This leads to the twelfth lesson on investing:

Investment Lesson #12: The key to successful investing is to focus on your ultimate goal of getting wealthy (or wealthier).

Understand What You Are Doing

The strategy must make sense to you, the investor. If something sounds too good to be true, it probably is. That saying is never truer than when applied to fly-by-night investment schemes. The underpinnings of an investment strategy should be understandable and logical.

You need to understand what is occurring with your money. Otherwise, you are abandoning your responsibility to yourself and the control that comes with it.

The problem with a lack of understanding arises when your investment portfolio starts to experience downturns. If you do not understand what is happening, you cannot determine if this is a short-term correction or a serious problem. If it continues, the pressure and pain can become intense, and they are magnified by this lack of knowledge. You start to make extremely unwise decisions that are driven by emotion because there is no basis to make a logical decision. I went through this myself and resolved never to do it again.

I saw this in the tech boom of the late 1990s. People invested in technology companies with no clue as to what they were doing. Remember the actions of Joe Investor in Chapter 1, as he is the perfect example. The great traders may have no knowledge about the stocks in which they invest, but they do have a discipline and set of rules for buying and selling.

This is the thirteenth lesson on investing:

Investment Lesson #13: Success with any investment strategy requires you, the investor, to understand it clearly and to have confidence in it.

Look for Superior but Realistic Rates of Return

As you read in Chapter 1 in the discussion between Joe Investor and his trusted accountant Ms. Advisor, beating the market as represented by the S&P 500 is incredibly difficult. Jack Bogle, founder of the multibillion-dollar mutual fund the Vanguard Group, found that only 2 to 5 percent of mutual funds beat the S&P 500 by more than 2 percent over an extended period of time. This means that only a very select few mutual funds have higher returns than 12.5 percent. Additional research has confirmed these findings to varying degrees. This bears repeating:

> Only 2 to 5 percent of mutual funds beat the S&P 500 by
> more than 2 percent over an extended period of time.[1]

What about those claims of incredible returns that you often see in advertisements? As we saw, they are usually referencing short time periods. However, because of the nature of capitalism, these bright returns usually fade to their dull reality as we extend the time frame.

What about those trading systems that seem to almost guarantee incredible wealth overnight? This may be true for a tiny group of individuals with nerves of steel and rapid-fire trading abilities. However, my experience is that most people, including myself, do not have these talents.

Let's face it: there is no free lunch. Instead of trying to double our money overnight, let's see if we can target returns in the 12 to 18 percent range. These returns are excellent, and they can be achieved over the long term.

Look for superior rates of return, by all means. Even when comparing similar types of investments, there is usually a wide range of performance. A solid investment strategy must outperform those with similar risks.

This is how real money is made, using the power of compound returns over time. As we extend the time horizon, even a 2 percent increase in the rate of return can make a tremendous difference in your wealth.

This leads us to the fourteenth lesson on investing:

Investment Lesson #14: Focus on achieving superior rates of returns that are realistic.

Understand Your Investment Time Frame

In the late 1990s, Warren Buffett decided not to participate in the large-cap growth technology boom that was dominating the market. His reason was that tech investing was not a strategy that he understood well enough to be assured that his participation would be a profitable experience.

As the tech rally continued and the performance of Mr. Buffett's investment vehicle, Berkshire Hathaway, lagged the market quite substantially, there were cries that he had lost his touch and that it might be time for him to retire. Many even whispered the ultimate insult at the time: "Buffett is a dinosaur who does not get it."

Remember, at the time his track record as an investor was virtually unmatched. He was able to maintain returns in excess of 20 percent over 30 years, but there were times during his career in which he had lagged the market in a similar fashion. In short, this period should not have been alarming to anyone who truly understood Mr. Buffett's track record and philosophy.

People who deserted him to participate in the tech rally without a clearly defined and researched investment strategy later regretted it. Berkshire Hathaway rallied as the tech bubble finally burst.

You have to get real on your investment time frame. You have to understand that any investment strategy will underperform during various periods.

There should be research that shows how the strategy performed over an extended period. This is why we take our Follow the Fed strategy research back to the 1920s before the Crash of 1929. This gives you the opportunity to see how the strategy would have performed over different market environments. Unless you want to be a day trader (and, trust me, you do not!), you need to assess your investment strategy's success over a time frame similar to your own.

This leads us to the fifteenth lesson on investing:

Investment Lesson #15: Any successful investment strategy will occasionally underperform, but it will work in the long run.

Understand Your Risk Tolerance

You should be at ease with the risk level of your portfolio. No investment or rate of return is worth an ulcer or worse. Money helps you enjoy your life. Do not allow your investment strategy to take that away from you.

Everyone is different. Getting the right split between fixed income and equity is sometimes as important as the correct equity strategy.

When a riskier strategy is going on all cylinders, it can appear to be easy money with no risk at all. This was the case with several hedge funds that invested in tech stocks in the late 1990s, right before they took a giant nosedive in value. During this time, I warned several people about the volatility of growth stocks, even the large established ones. They responded that they were long-term investors and were quite able to handle the volatility—often, with the hint of sarcasm in their voices for "people who just did not get it."

Unless these investments are part of a solid strategy and you are prepared for it, the level of pain can be massive and perhaps more than you can bear!

You are not going to enjoy the benefits of any investment strategy if you experience a heart attack or depression. Do not let greed push you over your own threshold of pain. Get real on your own level of risk tolerance.

This leads to the sixteenth lesson on investing:

Investment Lesson #16: Your tolerance for risk must match that of your investment strategy in order to be successful.

Remember the Power of Compounding

Remember The Edge? The Edge is the small increase in the return on your investment that allows you to reach your financial goals much faster. We are not talking about a get-rich-quick scheme. We are talking about minor increases in returns that can make substantial differences in your wealth over time.

This is the true key to getting wealthy. With the Follow the Fed strategy, you have to let the power of compounding work for you. The longer that you let it work, the more benefits it delivers. The great investors of the world always let the power of compounding work for them.

This leads to the seventeenth lesson of investing:

Investment Lesson #17: Without the power of compounding, an investment strategy will not succeed.

Understanding Yourself Is Key

I discussed how important it is to harmonize your investment strategy with your nervous system. However, this is only part of an even larger issue. You have to be comfortable with who you are. Becoming wealthy allows you to have the things you want, but it does not define you. It is a means to an end, not an end in itself.

If you are in a constant battle to keep up with the Jones, always competing and seeking their approval, it will be very difficult to stick with your investment strategy when it underperforms the market or when that next "big thing" comes around.

Don't be so hard on yourself. You do not need to be perfect to succeed. You just have to learn from your mistakes.

In my opinion, all the great investors know who they really are. They have the confidence to withstand peer pressure and media hype and to hold their ground through it all. Remember that the main reason that Joe Investor experienced those losses in Chapter 1 was a desire to be a player and not to miss an opportunity that Mr. Bigbucks had.

This leads to the eighteenth lesson on investing:

Investment Lesson #18: Understanding who you are is perhaps the most important requirement for investment success.

Get a Life

I have talked about the importance of remembering that wealth is a means to an end, not an end in itself. This is critical, particularly in sticking with a great investment strategy through the ups and downs and external pressures that will inevitably occur.

For most people investing is and should be a part-time activity. If you own a business or have a job, focus on that. How about your family and friends? If your business or job is not entirely satisfying, participate in a hobby or sport that is. Do not wait to get wealthy to start enjoying yourself. This is particularly true if you are retired.

At cocktail parties, you should be discussing your golf game, not obsessing about your investment strategy.

Warren Buffett attributes part of his success to the fact that he lives in Omaha instead of New York. He is isolated from the euphoria and depression that comes from New York's obsession with Wall Street. This allows him to prevent emotion from entering his decision-making process and so averts the chances of doing anything too stupid.

In 2007, Carlos Slim surpassed Bill Gates and Warren Buffett to become the richest man in the world.[2] Mr. Slim and his empire are all based in Mexico, far away from Wall Street.

Enjoy yourself and let the Follow the Fed do the work. It will make life a whole lot less stressful.

This leads to the nineteenth lesson on investing:

Investment Lesson #19: Having a life outside investing will dramatically decrease the stress of sticking with your investment strategy.

The Key Elements for Success: Self-Control and Commitment

We know The Edge is the small increase in the return on your investment that allows you to reach your financial goals over the long term. Our Follow the Fed strategy helps you get The Edge.

However, The Edge is useless if you do not have the self-control and commitment to implement and to stay with the strategies. My job is to try to make this easier for you to do. That is why I am explaining the strategies in detail. If I can take the anxiety out of investing, hopefully, it will be easier to control your emotions and to stick with the strategies.

Controlling emotions such as fear and greed is crucial, but it is entirely up to you to do that. I know that you can.

This is the twentieth lesson on investing:

Investment Lesson #20: Without self-control and commitment, successful investing is very difficult.

Getting Started

I have covered many of the things that you need to do to get wealthy or wealthier. However, all this knowledge will be useless unless you do one thing: "Get started!"

There is old saying about "paralysis by analysis." If you continue to study strategies and techniques *ad infinitum*, you will be waiting a long time. Nothing is absolutely certain; there is always risk in life, including getting up in the morning.

You must take the first step, even if it is small one. If you want, use the Follow the Fed strategy for only a portion of your portfolio. Just get started!

This is the twenty-first lesson on investing:

Investment Lesson #21: Action is required to make things happen in investing.

The Right Financial Advisor

The Follow the Fed strategy is simple and easy and is designed for an individual who wants to invest his money on his own with very little work. However, many people feel fearful and overwhelmed. They may not want to do it themselves and might want assistance from an investment professional.

This is one place where the right financial advisor can be helpful. He or she can assist you in implementing these strategies and sticking with them. Financial advisors need to be part of the solution, not the problem. They need to be concerned with keeping your costs low, not selling you expensive products.

Make sure that your advisor understands your philosophy and the Follow the Fed strategy and is willing to implement it. Your advisor must understand that you are in charge and that he or she is there to assist you, not to intimidate you.

This leads us to the twenty-second and final lesson of investing:

Investment Lesson #22: If you use a financial advisor, he or she must agree with your goals and philosophy and understand that you are in charge.

Summary

We covered the requirements for success, and from these came the final investment lessons. These lessons can be used to succeed with any investment strategy, as they are basic tenets that I found enhanced both my life and my net worth.

Investment Lesson #12: The key to successful investing is to focus on your ultimate goal of getting wealthy (or wealthier).

Investment Lesson #13: Success with any investment strategy requires you, the investor, to understand it clearly and to have confidence in it.

Investment Lesson #14: Focus on achieving superior rates of returns that are realistic.

Investment Lesson #15: Any successful investment strategy will occasionally underperform, but it will work in the long run.

Investment Lesson #16: Your tolerance for risk must match that of your investment strategy in order to be successful.

Investment Lesson #17: Without the power of compounding, an investment strategy will not succeed.

Investment Lesson #18: Understanding who you are is perhaps the most important requirement for investment success.

Investment Lesson #19: Having a life outside investing will dramatically decrease the stress of sticking with your investment strategy.

Investment Lesson #20: Without self-control and commitment, successful investing is very difficult.

Investment Lesson #21: Action is required to make things happen in investing.

Investment Lesson #22: If you use a financial advisor, he or she must agree with your goals and philosophy and understand that you are in charge.

These are *essential* lessons that I learned during my investment career. I made several mistakes myself, often with painful results. It is my intention to help you avoid these same pitfalls.

For a printable PDF download of the 22 lessons, visit www.FollowtheFedtheBook.com.

CHAPTER 7

The Secret to Beating the Market: Small Stocks

I have discussed the need to get The Edge in investing as the key to building long-term wealth. If you can get The Edge, that incremental level of outperformance above the market, then the law of compounding over time starts to operate heavily in your favor.

Since individual investors can take a long-term perspective, they actually can have an advantage over many of the large institutional investors. The institutions are often forced to have a short-term viewpoint because of performance pressures. If a mutual or hedge fund manager underperforms for a short period of time, he risks losing his investor base and the associated assets, despite a successful long-term track record. Many value managers learned this lesson the hard way, as they lost the funds they had under management when their performance lagged that of the growth managers in the late 1990s.

The Costs and Risks of Stockpicking

In Chapter 1, Joe learned that most managers and investors do not beat the market (as represented by the S&P 500). Jack Bogle, the founder of Vanguard Group, believes this is largely due to the high costs of stockpicking. With mutual funds, these fees and trading costs can amount to up to 2 percent a year or more.

There are many hidden costs when an investment manager buys and sells stocks:

- In seeking superior returns, a manager buying and selling stocks pays the bid–ask spread, or the difference between the buying and the selling price of shares.
- There are brokerage commissions involved in these transactions.
- Investors pay management fees (and possibly sales or load fees) to the fund manager.
- Managers are often competing with other managers with equal or superior skills at choosing stocks. It is a mathematical impossibility for everyone to do better than the market—for every dollar that outperforms the market average, some other investor's dollar must underperform.[1]

High levels of trading can cause unnecessary taxes as well. For example, if you sell stocks that are not in an IRA account, the difference between what you paid for the stock and what you sold it for is considered a capital gain. Depending on how much profit you made, this could put you into a higher tax bracket, causing you to pay higher income taxes.

Don't Try to Beat the Market

For years, before the popularity of mutual funds, the most common way to be involved in the stock market was the *buy-and-hold* strategy. This required you to pick some stocks of large companies that you liked (companies with $5 billion or more in market capitalizations, also known as blue chips) such as IBM or General Motors.[2] The strategy was to buy a reasonable amount of shares, sit back, and watch the money roll in. The idea was not to do anything fancy—just buy the big companies and wait.

With the development of mutual funds, you do not have to buy individual stocks—someone else does it for you. *Buy-and-hold* advocates suggest buying a low-cost market index fund (a mutual fund that tracks the performance of the S&P 500) instead. These funds usually have much cheaper management fees and provide tax advantages as well. Investors enjoy the benefits of long-term compounding that comes with investing in a diversified portfolio of large-cap stocks. This method is convenient, easy, and takes minimal time, especially when compared with trading stocks.

A Brief History of the Standard and Poor's 500 Index

The S&P 500 index is composed of 500 stocks that are considered a widely held sample of various industries in the United States. They are chosen by a committee from Standard and Poor's, a leading provider of information on the financial markets. Before 1957, the index consisted of only 90 of the largest stocks.

The S&P 500 index uses market value of the stocks and is generally considered one of the best measures of the U.S. stock market and a benchmark for mutual funds to be rated against.

Standard & Poor's traces its history back to 1860, with the publication by Henry Varnum Poor of *The History of Railroads and Canals in the United States.* This book was an attempt to compile comprehensive information about the financial and operational state of U.S. railroad companies. He went on to establish H.V. & H.W. Poor Co. with his son, Henry William, and published updated versions of this book on an annual basis.

The company as it is known today was formed in 1941 with the merger of Poor's Publishing (the successor company to H.V. and H.W. Poor Co.) and Standard Statistics. In 1966, S&P was acquired by The McGraw-Hill Companies and is now a part of the Financial Services division.[3]

Active Trading Is Even More Difficult

Stock trading presents a variety of potential problems. Time is of the essence when looking for those golden opportunities. Proper tools are required to watch these stocks, such as trade analysis software and real-time quote services. Time spent in front of the computer is a huge issue. For example, people with jobs need to be careful of the amount of time spent watching their stocks while at work. They are always looking over their shoulder, making sure the boss is not watching them. If they get caught, they could lose their jobs. The *buy-and-hold* strategy eliminates these problems.

The buy-and-hold strategy is great when the large-cap stocks are doing well—in times of a bull market. It also works if you are young enough to have a long enough time horizon not to worry short-term about the money you invested into the stock market. We all know that history has a habit of repeating itself. Historically, the market (S&P 500 and its predecessors) is up only about 10 percent per year from 1928 to 2006. For the *buy-and-hold* strategy to work, you need to believe that the market is going to go up over a long time period.

Is There a Better Way?

Stockpicking and active trading are the two most common, but still highly unlikely, ways to beat the S&P 500. Chapter 2 mentions people like Stevie Cohen, Jim Simons, and Warren Buffett, who can consistently beat the averages. However, as Ms. Advisor says in Chapter 1, it is difficult to find and then invest with such proven experts.

In order for The Edge to work, you need to be reasonably certain that the outperformance advantage will persist over time. Unfortunately, when looking for someone to advise you in your investing, it can be very difficult to differentiate between someone who knows a great stock and someone who just happens to be a great salesperson. I always felt that there had to be a better way.

In doing my research for Follow the Fed, I believed that the answer might be found by looking at the very nature of the market. The S&P 500 is simply a group of large stocks (in terms of market value) in the United States weighted by these capitalizations. The returns of the largest stocks massively influence the return of the index. However, there are other indices based on other characteristics, such as small stocks, growth stocks, and value stocks. I wondered if the answer might be found by looking at the performance of these indices.

The Definition of Value

Initially, based on the success of value investors like Ben Graham and Warren Buffett, I decided to examine a value stock index. However, when I began conducting my research, I found that there was no consistent definition of *value*. Some used simple ratios such as price-to-book value, price-to-earnings, price-to-cash flow, and price-to-sales. Others used more complex definitions, such as enterprise value (EV) or discounted cash flow (DCF).

In addition, there were very few value indices available that were tradable in the form of an index fund. Most value funds were actively managed. Although many of them were successful, most reflected the definition of "value" of the individuals managing them. This generally followed no consistent pattern upon which I could conduct extensive research.

An example is Bill Miller, the portfolio manager of the Legg Mason Value Trust, one of the most successful value mutual funds. During the late 1990s, much of its returns could be attributed to the performance of America Online (AOL). Other value managers claimed that this could not be considered a value stock under any conceivable definition. Mr. Miller disagreed and gave his own definition of value for AOL.

Based on these discrepancies, I decided to examine other factors that could form the basis of an index.

The Small Stocks Alternative

I decided to look at small-cap stocks, as the market capitalization of companies seemed to me a much more objective measure than value or growth. There also seemed to be several indices available to study, and an increasing number of index funds available that could serve as investment vehicles. Most had relatively low fee structures. These were stock indices whose companies had smaller market capitalizations, usually defined as ranging in market size from $250 million to $1 billion.[4]

In 1981, Rolf Banz, a graduate student at the University of Chicago, investigated the returns on stocks, using the database from the Center for Research in Security Prices (CRSP). He found that small stocks steadily outperformed large stocks, even after adjusting for risk.[5] Other economists and academics did additional research that supported his conclusions.

I found that small stocks offered higher rates of return over time. Statistics in Figure 7.1 and Table 7.1 show that these stocks tend to appreciate more than large stocks and are more risky as measured by volatility. However, the higher returns offered by small stocks nearly compensate for the additional volatility as indicated by a risk–return (Sharpe) ratio.

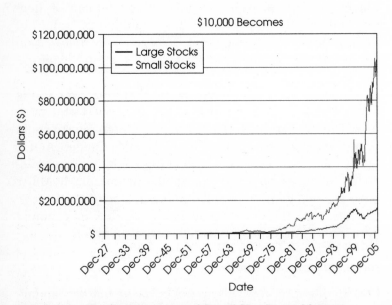

Figure 7.1 The Performance of Small Stocks and Large Stocks (1928 to 2006)

Table 7.1   Summary Return Results for Large Stocks and Small Stocks (1928 to 2006)

	Large[3]	Small[4]
Compound annual return	9.76%	12.47%
Risk (standard deviation of return)	0.1918	0.3722
Risk–return (Sharpe) ratio	0.4032	0.3887
Compound Annual Return by Decade		
1920s[1]	12.01%	–11.20%
1930s	–0.29%	2.94%
1940s	8.75%	19.91%
1950s	18.20%	19.04%
1960s	7.35%	15.38%
1970s	5.88%	8.77%
1980s	17.55%	12.11%
1990s	18.21%	13.96%
2000s[2]	1.13%	14.55%
$10,000 becomes:	$15,675,227	$107,597,565
Correlation to large stocks	1.0000	0.7789

Data drawn from the Kenneth R. French, Ph.D., Data Library (http://mba.tuck.dartmouth.edu/pages/faculty/ken.french/index.html) and Standard and Poor's (www.standardandpoors.com). Data current as of September 25, 2007.

Total holding period: January 1, 1928 to December 31, 2006
[1] January 1, 1928, to December 31, 1929
[2] January 1, 2000, to December 31, 2006
[3] Large Stock Index: 1928 to 1969 (Kenneth R. French, Ph.D., Data Library: Size Portfolio, Value Weighted Returns, Hi 20, Total Return), 1970–2006 (Standard and Poor's S&P 500 Total Return)
[4] Small Stock Index: Kenneth R. French, Ph.D., Data Library: Size Portfolio, Value Weighted Returns, Lo 20, Total Return.

The Type of Stock Is More Important than the Specific Stock, or, It's Not the House—It's the Neighborhood!

The interesting thing that I found during my research was that *the type of stock was much more important than the stock itself.* A diversified group of small stocks behaved very similarly when compared with large stocks. As long as the stock portfolio was large enough to achieve some diversification, the specific stocks seemed to be much less of a factor.

This is very similar to houses and neighborhoods. Have you ever seen a situation where the price of a beat-up house in a hot neighborhood skyrockets while a dream home in a less desirable area does nothing? For example, prices of waterfront property have gone through the roof, affecting nearly all properties in the surrounding areas. It is the same with stocks—if the company is in the right "neighborhood" it benefits from the momentum of others in the same category.

The Academic Research of Fama and French

The importance of size and market capitalization has been extensively studied since the initial academic inquiry performed in the early 1980s. Professors Eugene Fama of the University of Chicago and Kenneth French of Dartmouth College have been at the forefront of this research. Dr. Fama was the economist who coined the term *efficient markets* in the early 1960s.

In an article in the June 1992 edition of the *Journal of Finance*, "The Cross-Section of Expected Stock Returns," the two analyzed the importance of size of market capitalization (large vs. small) and book-to-market (growth vs. value) on stock market returns. They found that these two factors, along with the market itself, explained the significant portion of stock market returns.

The Small Stocks Advantage of the Early 2000s

This was illustrated by the performance of small stocks, especially those considered value picks, in the early 2000s.

This was after the crash when the Nasdaq 100 index fell 56.3 percent from the beginning of 2000 to the end of 2004, a 15.25 percent annual rate of loss. You would have done a lot better investing in a money market fund or bank savings account. Even Microsoft, the high-tech giant, was not a safe haven.

Table 7.2   Comparison of Returns, 2001 to 2005

Mutual Fund	Annual Return (2001–2005)
Russell 2000 Value	13.55%
DFA Small Cap Value	19.19%
DFA Micro	16.45%
Third Avenue Small Cap Value	12.46%
Vanguard S&P 500	0.41%

Source: Russell Investment Group, and Yahoo! Finance.

However, if you had invested in small value stocks, aside from the brief decline in 2002, you would have wondered why there was all of that talk about a bear market. Small-cap value mutual funds and exchange traded funds (ETF) did incredibly well during the first five years of the twenty-first century, especially compared to the S&P 500. See Table 7.2.

The 2.71 percent annual performance advantage of small stocks may not seem much of an edge (see Table 7.1). However, it is quite substantial when the mutual fund universe is analyzed for long-term performance.

Jack Bogle made a presentation at Washington State University in 2004, based on research in which he analyzed the performance of the 355 equity mutual funds that were in existence in 1970. After tracking this group's performance from 1970 to 2003, he found that only seven exceeded the return of the S&P 500 over that time by greater than 2 percent. This amounts to less than 2 percent of the original funds.[6]

I had found a better index than the S&P 500. It offered a performance advantage that was quite substantial when allowed to compound over time. There were several small stocks index funds available that could be used as an investment vehicle as well. Could it be that simple? Well, not so fast—as my research soon showed, there *are* exceptions that need to be taken into account, and they are big ones.

Dimensional Fund Advisors: Academic Theory in Practice

Academic research has often been criticized as having little practical application in the real world. The finance work of the academic community is said to be all theory. Before we accept this criticism at face value, we have to remember several key exceptions:

- The Vanguard Group's focus on market index funds was based on a research paper that Jack Bogle did as a student at Princeton University.
- Jim Simons, the hedge fund genius mentioned in Chapter 2, started as a math professor at the State University of New York.
- Ben Graham, the father of value investing and mentor of Warren Buffett, was a finance professor at Columbia University, as well as a partner in his own investment advisory firm.

Dimensional Fund Advisors, a Santa Monica, California, money management firm, was founded in the early 1980s as a way to put the research of Eugene Fama and Kenneth French (previously described) into practice. The firm's founders, David Booth and Rex Sinquefield, were both graduate students at the University of Chicago who studied under Dr. Fama.

Their first product was a small-cap index fund called the DFA 9-10 Fund (predecessor to the DFA Microcap Fund), which consisted of stocks of companies whose market capitalization put them in the New York Stock Exchange's bottom two deciles (the bottom 20 percent) when ranked by size.

Historically, many of the DFA funds have been top performers in their respective categories. The DFA funds also have a very low cost structure in terms of management fees and expenses versus actively managed funds.

Sources: Eric J. Savitz, "Ditching the Monkey," *Barron's Online* (January, 9, 2006); Joanna Ossinger, "The Dimensions of a Pioneering Strategy," *Wall Street Journal Online* (November 6, 2006).

Summary

I reviewed the costs and risks of stockpicking, provided a working definition of *value*, and examined the advantages of small stocks. The salient points from this chapter are the following:

- Stockpicking and active trading are extremely difficult methods to outperform the market as represented by the S&P 500 because of the tremendous costs involved.
- There are index funds that track indices other than the S&P 500.
- The long-term outperformance edge of small stocks has been demonstrated both in theory and in practice.

Continuing your research on small stocks means a visit to www.FollowtheFedtheBook.com, where you will find up-to-the-minute assessments of both small and large stocks.

The Catch with Small Stocks

As I pointed out in Chapter 7, I discovered that small stocks beat large stocks over an extended period. Therefore, there is good reason to believe that this is not a temporary phenomenon. There are a variety of low-cost index funds available to track this group of stocks, and most appear to possess the key ingredients of low management fees and expenses. This performance advantage also appears to be quite significant when compared to the long-term performance of mutual funds that invest in the stock market. It would appear that we have discovered a simple, secret solution to beating the market (and most professional investors).

Investing in small stocks is profitable but not necessarily that easy. There are some problems of which you should be aware before you invest your entire portfolio in a small stocks index fund. All opportunities usually have risks associated with them, and in this case, the outperformance advantage of small stocks has a few that you need to know.

Devastating Drawdowns in Bear Markets

Small stocks can severely underperform large stocks during bear markets. The truly severe bear markets are scary enough if you are invested in large stocks, but they can be absolutely terrifying if you own small stocks. Some long-term investors believe they can deal with this situation.

My view is that this is possible but very difficult. During the bear market of the early 2000s, I saw several long-term investors panic when the pain of losing money became too great.

Bear markets are a valid concern, given the uncertainty and high valuation in the market today. Grandparents and great-grandparents remember the decade of the 1930s as one of the worst economic times in history—the Great Depression. Economic growth was low, unemployment was extremely high, and the future looked grim. This crash will live forever in their minds. On October 28 and 29, 1929, Wall Street saw the largest percentage drop in history. The Dow Jones Industrial Average (DJIA) plunged from 301.22 to 260.64 on Black Monday, a 13.5 percent drop in one day. It fell to 230.07 on Black Tuesday, for a combined loss of 23.6 percent. It took 35 years for the Dow to recover.[1]

Let us compare the performance of large stocks and small stocks during the Great Depression in Table 8.1. Although large stocks lost almost two-thirds of their value

Table 8.1 Performance During the Great Depression

Year	Large Stocks	Small Stocks
1929	−8.90%	−47.85%
1930	−27.15%	−48.14%
1931	−42.75%	−52.85%
1932	−9.38%	8.86%
1929–1932	**−65.57%**	**−86.12%**
1933	50.42%	151.81%
1934	2.92%	35.18%
1935	44.18%	72.29%
1936	30.77%	76.02%
1929–1936	**0.52%**	**43.30%**

Source: Data drawn from the Kenneth R. French, Ph.D., Data Library (http://mba.tuck.dartmouth.edu/pages/faculty/ken.french/index.html) and Standard and Poor's (www.standardandpoors.com). Data current as of September 25, 2007.

between 1929 and 1932, small stocks lost even more. However, small stocks strongly outperformed for most of the next four years (1933–1936) and actually outperformed over the entire period. The real question was whether you had the intestinal fortitude to stay invested for the rebound.

We find a similar situation in the late 1960s, the 1970s, and the early 1980s (see Table 8.2). Small stocks lost almost 70 percent of their value from 1969 to 1974, but large stocks lost substantially less. However, this was on the eve of one of the greatest small-stock booms in history that made up for all the underperformance. The question was whether you would still have been *in* small stocks to realize these gains.

Table 8.2 Performance from 1969 to 1983

Year	Large Stocks	Small Stocks
1969	−7.02%	−31.32%
1970	3.94%	−17.63%
1971	14.30%	17.93%
1972	19.00%	0.24%
1973	−14.69%	−38.21%
1974	−26.47%	−27.24%
1969–1974	**−17.54%**	**−69.93%**
1975	37.23%	59.11%
1976	23.93%	48.60%
1977	−7.16%	27.48%
1978	6.57%	24.63%
1979	18.61%	40.94%
1980	32.50%	39.99%
1981	−4.92%	−1.67%
1982	21.55%	27.75%
1983	22.56%	34.17%
1969–1983	**208.84%**	**275.54%**

Source: Data drawn from the Kenneth R. French, Ph.D., Data Library (http://mba.tuck.dartmouth.edu/pages/faculty/ken.french/index.html) and Standard and Poor's (www.standardandpoors.com). Data current as of September 25, 2007.

Investor Returns Are Less than Mutual Fund Returns

In his research, Jack Bogle discovered that mutual fund investors not only underperformed the market but also underperformed the underlying mutual funds themselves by over 3 percent during 1984 to 2004. The costs, fees, and commissions paid for trading already underperforming mutual funds only compounded the losses.

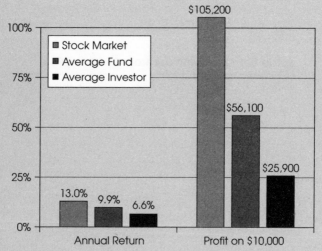

The Stock Market, The Average Equity Fund, and the Average Equity Fund Investor: 1984–2004

Based on my observations of investor behavior, I believe that this could be largely due to emotions of greed and fear getting the best of investors.

Source: Bogle Financial Markets Research Center, "In Investing, You Get What You Pay For," Remarks by John C. Bogle, founder and former chairman, Vanguard Group, The World Money Show, Orlando, Florida, February 2, 2005, www.vanguard.com.

Sustained Underperformance Relative to the S&P 500

Small stocks can also be out of sync with large stocks, as they were in the late 1990s when optimism was high. In 1999, debt levels hit a record high in almost every category: corporate, consumer, and mortgage debt markets. Margin debt (the ability to purchase stock on 50 percent credit) ballooned.[2] In 1999, one of the economists even boldly stated that the economy would continue to grow forever and that "recessions are a thing of the past."[3] Little did he know!

At the time there was incredible demand for stocks of large technology companies. New Internet-based companies were popping up everywhere, and their stocks were highly overvalued.

During the late 1980s and 1990s, small stocks underperformed the S&P 500 quite severely. For the 10 years from 1986 to 1995, small stocks underperformed large stocks with an annual return of 8.6 percent compared to 14.9 percent. This was quite a reversal of the small stocks' outperformance of the late 1970s and early 1980s. There was a short period from 1991 to 1993 when small stocks rallied, leading some people to predict that a new small-stocks cycle was beginning.

However, just as people were predicting the rebirth of small stocks, the large stocks rally increased in strength. From 1996 to 1999, small stocks had a compound annual return of 16.9 percent compared to large stocks return of 26.4 percent. Small stocks investors were getting crushed. Many people I knew abandoned these stocks just in time for a new small stocks rally to really begin.

I witnessed firsthand the pain that this inflicted on the average investor. Since many of these people had no real investment strategy, switching to a tactic based on panic not only caused severe stress but also inflicted substantial damage on their portfolios. It was a tremendous lesson.

We also saw this pattern in the two charts above showing the effects of the two most severe bear markets in recent history and the subsequent recoveries.

The Financial Strength of Large Stocks

There is a certain comfort in the financial strength of large companies. They are seasoned and usually have greater financial resources than small companies. Perhaps you have heard someone say that a company such as General Electric or Merck is just simply too large to go bankrupt. During troubled times, people comfort themselves that these *blue-chip* companies will emerge as survivors, and that the same cannot be said of smaller companies. That is why people tend to gravitate to larger stocks.

Research analysts often follow large companies, providing an additional form of validation for the average investor. An investor may feel that if Wall Street covers them, there is no doubt that they will be around. However, it is far from the truth—take companies like Enron, Polaroid, and MCI, for example.

Lastly, when investors go to a cocktail party or social event, they are more likely to feel comfortable talking about their latest investment in Microsoft than a small company that no one knows. I saw this phenomenon present in many social situations during the late 1990s. You are also more likely to see these larger companies covered on television and in other financial media.

The Concentration of Small Stock Outperformance

An interesting pattern can be seen in Figure 7.1 and Table 7.1 from Chapter 7. In certain decades, small stocks outperformed (1930s, 1940s, 1950s, 1960s, 1970s, and 2000s), and in others, large stocks outperformed (1920s, 1980s, and 1990s).

During the periods of 1931 to 1935, 1941 to 1945, and 1975 to 1983, large stocks massively underperformed small stocks. From 1931 to 1945, small companies had great returns near the bottom of the Great Depression. These stocks moved up more than 100 percent, easily whipping

Research on Small Stock Outperformance: The Wharton School at the University of Pennsylvania

Jeremy Siegel, a professor at the Wharton School at the University of Pennsylvania, found that between 1975 and the end of 1983, small stocks exploded. They averaged a 35.3 percent compounded annual return, more than double the 15.7 percent return on large stocks. Total returns on small stocks during these nine years exceeded 1,400 percent. He also found that if you exclude this period from the returns of large stocks and small stocks from 1926 to 2001, large caps outperform.[4]

Small Stocks and S&P 500 Returns, 1926 to 2001	S&P 500	Small Stocks
Including 1975–1983	10.53%	12.27%
Excluding 1975–1983	9.84%	9.49%

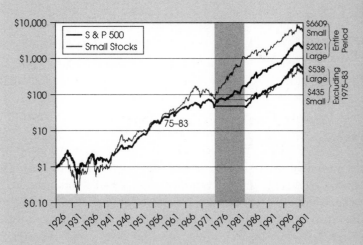

Source: Jeremy Siegel, *Stocks for the Long Run* (New York: McGraw-Hill, 2002). Reproduced with the permission of the McGraw-Hill Companies.

their larger brethren.[5] From 1941 to 1945, the market was lacking both cash and assets, but small stocks still rose, leaving the investors extremely happy with their giant pay-offs.[6]

Small stocks' outperformance is concentrated in incredibly short periods. If you miss these periods, Dr. Siegel's research demonstrates that the small stocks' advantage disappears. This is not an easy situation, which may be the main reason why this phenomenon continues to persist. You are underperforming the S&P 500 for a long time, until finally your portfolio blasts off like a rocket ship. If you panic during the underperformance phase or are not around for this brief period of outperformance, then your portfolio can be decimated in the same way that Jack Bogle's research illustrates the average mutual fund investor underperforms the average fund.

Some have criticized the Siegel study for picking a specific period that justifies his conclusion, but I disagree with these critics. At the Channel Capital Research Institute, LLC, we conducted additional research that ultimately supports Dr. Siegel's work and his conclusion.

As part of my research, I analyzed the period from 1928 to 2006. If you exclude the five years with the highest returns for small stocks, you find that they had a compound annual return of 8.08 percent versus large stocks with a return of 8.41 percent. The small stocks' performance advantage disappears. See Figures 8.1 and 8.2, as well as Table 8.3.

I cannot be accused of selecting these years to support my conclusion. I simply picked the years with the highest returns. These five years (1933, 1936, 1943, 1945, and 1967) were not concentrated in any particular period, with the exception of the two years during World War II. However, this additional research illustrates the problem of short-term small stocks' outperformance that I mentioned.

The small stocks advantage that I described in Chapter 7 definitely has some problems associated with it. However, by using the Follow the Fed strategy, I discovered a way to counter some of these issues.

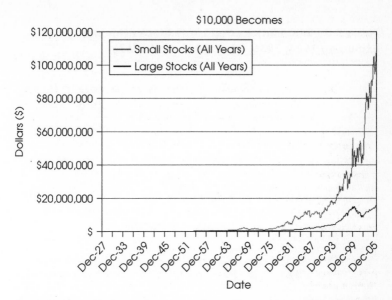

Figure 8.1   The Performance of Small Stocks and Large Stocks (1928–2006)

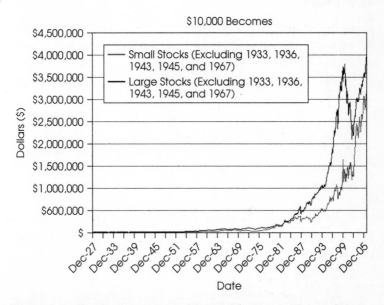

Figure 8.2   The Performance of Small Stocks and Large Stocks (1928–2006 excluding 1933, 1936, 1943, 1945, and 1967)

Table 8.3   Small Stocks and Large Stocks (Including and Excluding 1933, 1936, 1943, 1945, and 1967)

	Small Stocks[1] Including	Large Stocks[2] Including	Small Stocks[1] Excluding	Large Stocks[2] Excluding
Compound Annual Return	12.47%	9.76%	8.08%	8.41%
$10,000 becomes:	$107,597,565	$15,675,227	$3,152,203	$3,948,472

Source: Data drawn from the Kenneth R. French, Ph.D., Data Library (http://mba.tuck.dartmouth.edu/pages/faculty/ken.french/index.html) and Standard and Poor's (www.standardandpoors.com). Data current as of September 25, 2007.

Total Holding Period: January 1, 1928 to December 31, 2006.
[1]Small Stock Index: Kenneth R. French, Ph.D., Data Library: Size Portfolio, Value Weighted Returns, Lo 20, Total Return.
[2]Large Stock Index: 1928–1969 (Kenneth R. French, Ph.D., Data Library: Size Portfolio, Value Weighted Returns, Hi 20, Total Return), 1970–2006 (Standard and Poor's S&P 500 Total Return).

Summary

Investing in small stocks is profitable but not necessarily easy. All opportunities usually have risks associated with them:

- Small stocks vastly underperform and can have huge drawdowns during severe bear markets.
- Small-stock underperformance can last for long periods.
- The small-stock outperformance advantage is usually concentrated in short periods with spectacular returns.

Visit www.FollowtheFedtheBook.com for resources and up-to-the-minute assessments of stock performance and market activities.

CHAPTER 9

The Big Question: Why Do Small Stocks Outperform?

I have documented the outperformance of small stocks over large stocks in the last 79 years. The difference is quite substantial: $10,000 invested in small stocks in 1928 would have turned into more than $107 million by 2006, while the same investment in large stocks would have reached little more than $15.5 million.

However, I have also discussed the issues associated with investing in small stocks: the devastating drawdowns in bear markets, the sustained underperformance relative to the S&P 500, the financial strength of large stocks, and the concentration of small stocks' outperformance in extremely brief periods of time. The demand for higher returns because of these problems may be why the small stocks' outperformance advantage has persisted for so long. This raises the broader issue of why its advantage continues.

The Efficient Markets Explanation

Proponents of efficient markets claim that it is impossible to beat the market. They contend that the financial players analyze all available information, which is then factored into equity prices based on the competitive bidding nature of the stock market. Therefore, it is virtually impossible to get greater than the fair return on your investment because there is too much competition from other financial players.

There are several different schools of efficient market theorists. Some claim that all publicly available information is discounted into stock prices. There are differing opinions as to how long this process takes. Some say that the reaction to new information is instantaneous, while others say that this takes place over time. However, using these temporary inefficiencies to make money on a consistent basis is extremely difficult and virtually impossible for the average investor.

If the stock market is truly efficient, how do the efficient-markets proponents explain the performance advantage of small stocks? This is not a temporary anomaly that disappears relatively quickly. I have shown that it has persisted from 1928 to 2006 and has occurred repeatedly during this period.

Their answer lies in the definition of efficient markets, which allows for higher returns for higher levels of risk. The S&P 500 has higher returns over time when compared with those of U.S. Treasury bills. However, stocks have a higher level of risk when compared to the debt obligation of the U.S. government.

This explanation has a certain level of validity if you define risk as *volatility*. Small stocks are more volatile than large stocks. In Table 7.1 in Chapter 7, you see that small stocks have a standard deviation of return (a measure of volatility) of 0.3722, which is substantially higher than 0.1918 of large stocks. Small stocks have a lower risk–return ratio (also known as a Sharpe ratio) of 0.3887 versus 0.4032 for large stocks, although the difference is minimal.

Moreover, efficient-markets advocates do not have an explanation for why the small-stock outperformance advantage seems to be concentrated in short periods.

Explanation of Irrational Mr. Market

Warren Buffett and his mentor, Ben Graham, often mentioned the irrationality of the stock market. This has allowed value investors like themselves to earn above-average returns with no real additional risk. They actually refer to the stock market as if it was an actual person and call it "Mr. Market."

Mr. Market has a manic-depressive personality. One day he is happy, and the next he is sad. This is reflected in the differing prices that he offers for the stocks that he sells, sometimes with no correlation to the actual value. By using Mr. Market's apparent irrationality to one's advantage, an investor can achieve above-average investment returns.

This was used as an explanation for the underpricing of value stocks but can also be used to explain small stocks as well. In Chapter 8, I mentioned the comfort of large companies' financial strength. It is much easier to discuss and, therefore, to invest in Microsoft or General Electric than a small company that no one really knows.

However, Mr. Market does not give us an explanation for the concentration of the outperformance advantage. People are not irrational and then suddenly rational for short periods in cycles.

The Availability of Wall Street Information

The availability of Wall Street information is yet another explanation for the small stocks' advantage. Many Wall Street professionals follow larger companies and pass their "wisdom" on to the investors. Small stocks often do not have this advantage in distributing information. Thus, investors often overlook or ignore the attractiveness of certain small companies.

When I attended an analyst meeting about General Electric several years ago, there were more than 100 investment professionals in the room. This included buy-side analysts, sell-side analysts, portfolio managers, investment bankers, and journalists. Each had a cell phone and was conveying the information almost instantaneously to colleagues back at headquarters and, in some cases, directly to their best clients. All of these people seemed bright and intelligent and quite capable of analyzing the data and information as well as I could. In such an environment, it was extremely difficult to get an edge over the person next to you.

Such information is even more easily distributed now. Some companies give live Webcasts over the Internet and may even broadcast the information directly over television. Often, these meetings are conducted in New York to attract more Wall Street professionals.

Any new information from the large companies usually hits the airwaves instantly. The news is carried at the top of the business sections of major newspapers and magazines. You also see it directly on the major news services on the Internet.

Distribution of information for small companies is quite different. Since many of these companies are off the beaten path, it may be extremely difficult to get to their corporate headquarters. It may involve a multiday trip to visit and to get access to valuable information. With large companies, there is usually an entire investor relations department and staff. By contrast, small companies usually have only one investor relations person, who may be a secretary or administrator with other responsibilities.

I have found that getting information from some of the small companies is like pulling teeth. After all, their primary responsibility is to operate the business, not to promote the stock.

You also have to look at the nature of Wall Street itself. As I mentioned in the Introduction, the investment firms are businesses first and operate to generate a profit. They benefit by covering large companies because they are potential sources of future investment-banking business. Also, the customers of the sales and trading divisions of these firms demand coverage of the large companies, which are, after all, the ones that generate the most commissions.

These conditions usually do not exist with small companies. After the initial public offering (IPO), many small companies do not return to the investment banks for years. The banks' sales and trading customers usually do not need analysts' coverage because they may not be aware of the existence of these companies, whose small-stock trading may not repay the costs of research.

Although it is interesting, this information disparity does not explain the unique pattern of outperformance of small stocks.

The Real Answer: The Availability of Money and Credit

Another major difference between large and small companies is the availability of money and credit. Without adequate financing, it is extremely difficult for a company to grow and to generate a satisfactory return on its investment. This also means the performance of the stock will suffer as well.

Large companies such as General Electric usually do not have problems raising money, except under the most extreme circumstances. They can access the debt and the equity markets, as well as private sources and banks. Only the *cost* of borrowing changes over time. Money is available even during hard times, albeit at a higher interest rate.

Small companies are in a different situation. Accessing the public debt and equity markets is extremely difficult because of the high costs involved. Relative to the amount of money raised, these costs can be quite overwhelming. Bank loans or small private placements are usually the easier option but are still quite expensive.

I have experienced both sides. I saw what was involved with corporate finance for the large companies when I was an investment banker in Morgan Stanley's New York and London offices. However, I saw the opposite side of the equation when I grew my own business and was dependent on money and credit from others.

In the periods of small stocks' outperformance, money and credit seemed to be incredibly easy to obtain from the banks. For the first time, I noticed some type of an explanation for the small stocks' outperformance pattern. Wall Street was finally starting to make sense.

From 1931 to 1935, the Federal Reserve (Fed) was trying to help pull the country out of the Depression. Initially, the Fed increased interest rates dramatically to reduce the growth in money supply. This slowed the economy and hurt corporate profits. Deep into the Depression, the Fed actually reversed course and reduced interest rates on government bonds and corporate debt.[1] This massively increased liquidity, and a huge small-stock rally began.

In the early 1940s, Wall Street was not the force it had once been. Franklin D. Roosevelt was president, and World War II was hanging over the country's head. The U.S. Treasury mounted massive bond drives, selling bonds in both large and small denominations to everyone, including schoolchildren. The U.S. Treasury needed to raise over $59 billion for the war effort. Liquidity was vital, so the government poured money into the economy, enabling people to buy war bonds.[2] Again small stocks benefited.

During 1975 to 1983, the country was dealing with an oil crisis. Until Paul Volcker took over as chairman of the Fed, monetary policy was relatively loose, with money easy to borrow. This was the period that Jeremy Siegel cited in his research as the greatest small-stocks boom in recent history.

Most recently, after the catastrophe at the World Trade Center on September 11, 2001, the Fed accelerated lowering of the federal funds rate, injecting money into the economy. The mantra then was, "Go out and spend money! Go to the movies, dine out, and buy that car you were thinking about." During that tumultuous period, the Fed's top priority was to make enough money and credit available to keep the economy going. For the next several years, borrowing money became quite easy for small companies. As I documented in Chapter 7, small stocks substantially outperformed during this period.

Measurement of Easy Money and Credit: Follow the Fed

The Fed is one of the main institutions that determine interest rates and, consequently, the availability of easy money and credit. This is the source of the popular expression on Wall Street, "Don't Fight the Fed."

The Fed has a variety of tools at its disposal to affect monetary policy and interest rates. When money supply expands, banks receive more money, giving them more lending power. Often, this abundance is made available to small companies for investment and expansion. Interest rates affect corporate earnings. The more interest a company pays, the lower its profit.

Summary

As we saw earlier, the Fed's power to influence the economy is massive. Similar patterns existed before the Fed with the banks of the robber barons able to set the terms of financing for smaller companies. However, the scale became much larger with the creation of the Fed.

The question is how to measure this infusion of money and credit by the Fed and how to link it successfully to the small stocks' outperformance cycle.

I reviewed the most commonly proposed explanations for the small stocks outperformance advantage:

- Efficient markets advocates claim that small stocks' outperformance advantage is merely compensation for a higher level of risk for the investor.
- Irrational markets theorists say that it is merely an opportunity for astute investors to take advantage of inherent inefficiencies in the equity markets.
- Because coverage and analysis of small companies by Wall Street firms is less than large companies, there are greater opportunities for higher investor returns.
- The availability of money and credit are more important factors for small stocks than large stocks. This is largely under the control of the Federal Reserve.

I concluded that the Federal Reserve's monetary policy and interest rates drive the small stock advantage.

Continuing your research means a visit to www. FollowtheFedtheBook.com, where you will find up-to-the-minute assessments of stock performance.

CHAPTER

10

Proving the Follow the Fed Formula for Small Stocks

There are many things that influence the returns of small stocks, but the availability of money and credit is the primary factor in their long-term outperformance. In today's world, the U.S. Federal Reserve is the primary institution that drives this availability. There are other institutions involved, but in comparison, the Fed's power dwarfs all others. As I mentioned earlier, this led to the expression on Wall Street, "Don't Fight the Fed."

So, the question is, how do we measure this power? How do we use it to determine when small stocks are likely to outperform large stocks? We need to test this over a sufficiently long period with varying economic conditions to make sure that the results are not unique to a particular time.

This reduces the chances that my strategy is only useful for a limited period. I believe that this is one of the reasons why many quantitative investment strategies sometimes explode when put into practice. They are developed using only a few years' data, which may include a period when conditions seem to vindicate their theory. Then, when the strategy is put into practice, conditions change, and the strategy no longer works.

The formula that we use to determine if we should invest in small stocks or large stocks should be simple to understand

and easy to implement. The concept of the *simple solution being the best solution* has been known for many years. In 1320, William of Occam expressed it best when he said, "Entities should not be multiplied unnecessarily." This concept came to be known as *Occam's Razor*.

My Follow the Fed strategy is simple. Loose money and credit conditions will favor small stocks, while tight money and credit conditions will favor large stocks.

Direction of Interest Rates

The most common technique used to measure the availability of money and credit is the direction of interest rates. If interest rates are rising, then monetary and credit conditions are said to be tightening. By contrast, if they are falling, then conditions are said to be loosening.

The Fed's primary method of influencing this is raising or lowering (often referred to as *tightening* or *loosening* the monetary policy) the *discount and federal funds rates*. The discount rate is the rate at which the Fed lends to member banks, and the federal funds rate is the rate at which banks lend to each other. (There is additional information in the Glossary and Appendix at the end of this book.)

Marty Zweig, noted author, economist, and investor, has developed formulas to quantify the Fed's movements on interest rates. In these formulas, it sometimes takes larger or multiple moves by the Fed to change from loose to tight or tight to loose money and credit conditions. These formulas were previously used to determine the likelihood of a bear market.

I have examined the direction of interest rates and have found they were not sufficient to explain the relationship between small stocks and large stocks (see Table 10.1). During the late 1970s and early 1980s, interest rates were rising quite dramatically, indicating supposedly tightening conditions. However, this was also one of the greatest small-stock bull markets in history, and during much of the 1980s, interest rates were falling. However, large stocks outperformed small stocks for most of this period. What was going on?

Table 10.1 Performance of Large and Small Stocks in Relation to Treasury Bills

Year	Large Stocks	Small Stocks	U.S. Treasury Bills
1976	23.93%	48.60%	4.97%
1977	–7.16%	27.48%	5.27%
1978	6.57%	24.63%	7.19%
1979	18.61%	40.94%	10.07%
1980	32.50%	39.99%	11.43%
1981	–4.92%	–1.67%	14.03%
1982	21.55%	27.75%	10.61%
1983	22.56%	34.17%	8.61%
1984	6.27%	–10.42%	9.52%
1985	31.73%	28.94%	7.48%
1986	18.67%	3.70%	5.98%
1987	5.25%	–14.06%	5.78%

Source: Data drawn from the Kenneth R. French, Ph.D., Data Library (http://mba.tuck.dartmouth.edu/pages/faculty/ken.french/index.html), Standard and Poor's (www.standardandpoors.com), and the Federal Reserve Bank of St. Louis—three-month T-bill. Data current as of September 25, 2007.

Other Methods to Influence Money and Credit

The Fed has other means of influencing money and credit conditions. This includes open-market transactions in which the Fed buys or sells government debt in the form of U.S. Treasuries, which injects money into the banking system. It can also set margin requirements, which determine the amount that investors can borrow when purchasing stocks and bonds. Additional information on these other methods can be found in the Appendix at the end of the book. However, I found that none of these methods could sufficiently explain the outperformance of small stocks.

I also examined the influence of the other central banks, such as the European Central Bank (ECB), but found no discernable correlation. Although these central banks definitely exerted influence, the Fed's power and scale were much larger. I found that most of these central banks' policies were actually influenced by the Federal Reserve. The Fed did not directly control these central banks but was "first among equals."

Fedspeak: The Difference between What the Fed *Says* and *Does*

I examined all the methods that the Fed used to influence money and credit. Although I could explain conceptually why small stocks outperformed and how the Fed influenced the situation, I could not develop a simple formula that allowed me to test this. It was becoming quite discouraging.

Then, I finally achieved a breakthrough in my analysis. As I was watching testimony before Congress by former Fed Chairman Alan Greenspan, I suddenly realized that I had not the slightest idea what he was saying. At first, I thought that maybe I had missed something. However, after watching the representatives on television question him, it appeared that many of them did not seem to have a clue, either. After the testimony, television commentators and various Fed experts tried to analyze the testimony, and their understanding seemed to be lacking as well. I only hoped that at least Dr. Greenspan understood what he was saying.

Then, I realized that separating the "news" from the "noise," when it comes to Fed policy, is very difficult. Sometimes the statements are unclear and often have very little relation to what the Fed actually does. The most important thing to watch is not what the Fed *says* but what it *does*.

Former Chairman Greenspan let the truth about *Fedspeak* out in his new book, *The Age of Turbulence.* It seems that this confusion was intentional on his part and was meant to prevent unintended jolts to the financial markets from Fed comments. The success of Fedspeak in accomplishing this goal will be the source of heated debate for a long time.

In any case, I began to focus less on the Fed's formal actions and more on the underlying economic conditions. This way, I could see what the Fed was actually doing.

Inflation: Large Stocks versus Small Stocks

I noticed that during two periods of small-stock outperformance, inflation was rampant. During the early 1940s, World War II was being fought, and during the mid-to-late 1970s and early 1980s, oil prices were kept quite high by the restrictive policies of OPEC. It is easy to see why inflation was a factor.

Inflation is generally considered to be bad for stocks. I decided to examine its impact on small stocks and large stocks separately. See Table 10.2.

Based on generally accepted assumptions, the results were not what I expected. Large stocks were negatively impacted by inflation in the short term, but there was virtually no correlation in the long term. However, the effect of inflation on small stocks was less negative in the short term and actually positive in the long term.

Small stocks benefited more from inflation, while large stocks did not. This makes intuitive sense. Smaller companies can adjust to changing economic conditions much more quickly than larger companies. It is like trying to steer a speedboat versus a battleship. One turns on a dime, while the other may require several miles to change course. The same is true with businesses.

The Solution: Real Interest Rates

I decided to analyze another period of small-stock outperformance—the mid-1930s. The country was just beginning

Table 10.2 Correlation of Inflation with Large Stocks and Small Stocks

Inflation Correlation	1972–2006	1928–2006
Large Stocks	–0.164	0.005
Small Stocks	–0.122	0.018

Source: Data drawn from the Kenneth R. French, Ph.D., Data Library (http://mba. tuck.dartmouth.edu/pages/faculty/ken.french/index.html), Standard and Poor's (www.standardandpoors.com), and the U.S. Department of Labor: Bureau of Labor Statistics (www.bls.gov/cpi/home.htm). Data current as of September 25, 2007.

to emerge from the Great Depression. The liquidity that the Fed had been injecting into the economy was starting to take effect, and small stocks began to rally.

However, there was a problem. Inflation during this time was minimal. The Great Depression was a deflationary period. Nonetheless, there was still plenty of excess capacity for economic growth as the country emerged from this economic slump, and interest rates were virtually zero.

I noticed something very interesting for all three periods: For most of them, the interest rate on U.S. Treasury bills was less than the rate of inflation. Real interest rates (interest rates adjusted for the rate of inflation; see Table 10.3) were negative. This was the magic formula that I had been seeking.

Table 10.3   Real Rates of Interest

Year	U.S. Treasury Bills	Inflation	U.S. Treasury Bills (Real Rates)
Great Depression			
1934	0.28%	1.52%	−1.22%
1935	0.17%	2.98%	−2.73%
1936	0.17%	1.45%	−1.26%
World War II			
1942	0.34%	9.03%	−7.97%
1943	0.38%	2.96%	−2.51%
1944	0.38%	2.30%	−1.88%
1945	0.38%	2.25%	−1.83%
The 1970s Oil Crisis			
1975	5.78%	6.94%	−1.08%
1976	4.97%	4.86%	0.10%
1977	5.27%	6.70%	−1.34%
1978	7.19%	9.02%	−1.68%
1979	10.07%	13.29%	−2.84%
1980	11.43%	12.52%	−0.97%
The 2000s Rally			
2002	1.60%	2.38%	−0.76%
2003	1.01%	1.88%	−0.85%
2004	1.37%	3.26%	−1.83%
2005	3.15%	3.42%	−0.26%

Test of the Follow the Fed Standard Strategy

As I mentioned previously, small stocks outperform *when money and credit are easily obtained.* This seems to be best indicated when real, short-term interest rates are negative. You are essentially borrowing money for free. This occurs when short-term Treasury bill rates are essentially less than the rate of inflation. This information can easily be obtained from various public sources. If you invest only in small stocks when this occurs, you would have achieved a return of 12.47 percent from 1928 to 2006, compared to 9.76 percent for a buy-and-hold strategy for large stocks, as shown in Figure 10.1 and Table 10.4. Only 35 trades would have been generated over a 79-year period—a trade about every 2.3 years.

If you track this data on a monthly basis, even with a two-month lag, this leaves you plenty of time to go on vacation and enjoy your life while still potentially achieving market-beating returns. There are some whipsaws—situations in

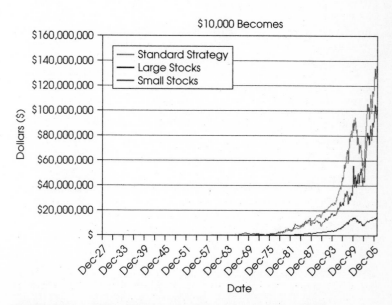

Figure 10.1 Performance of Follow the Fed Standard Strategy, Large Stocks and Small Stocks (1928 to 2006)

Table 10.4   Summary Return Results for Follow the Fed Standard Strategy: Large and Small Stocks (1928 to 2006)

	Standard Strategy	Large[3]	Small[4]
Compound annual return	12.85%	9.76%	12.47%
Risk (standard deviation of return)	0.2848	0.1918	0.3722
Return–risk (Sharpe) ratio	0.4403	0.4032	0.3887
Number of trades	35	–	–
Compound Annual Return by Decade			
1920s[1]	12.01%	12.01%	−11.20%
1930s	−1.24%	−0.29%	2.94%
1940s	18.97%	8.75%	19.91%
1950s	18.58%	18.20%	19.04%
1960s	7.35%	7.35%	15.38%
1970s	14.92%	5.88%	8.77%
1980s	19.48%	17.55%	12.11%
1990s	18.44%	18.21%	13.96%
2000s[2]	6.38%	1.13%	14.55%
$10,000 becomes:	$ 140,098,806	$ 15,675,227	$ 107,597,565
Correlation to large stocks	0.8858	1.0000	0.7789

Source: Data drawn from Kenneth R. French, Ph.D., Data Library (http://mba.tuck. dartmouth.edu/pages/faculty/ken.french/index.html) and Standard and Poor's (www.standardandpoors.com). Data current as of September 25, 2007. Actual live signals issued from ChannelCapitalResearch.com were used for 2006.

Total holding period: January 1, 1928, to December 31, 2006.
[1] January 1, 1928, to December 31, 1929.
[2] January 1, 2000, to December 31, 2006.
[3] Large Stock Index: 1928 to 1969 (Kenneth R. French, Ph.D., Data Library: Size Portfolio, Value Weighted Returns, Hi 20, Total Return), 1970–2006, and Standard and Poor's S&P 500 Total Return.
[4] Small Stock Index: Kenneth R. French, Ph.D., Data Library: Size Portfolio, Value Weighted Returns, Lo 20, Total Return.

which the Standard Follow the Fed Strategy generates a signal and then quickly reverses itself, possibly generating a loss because of trading costs or taxes. A *whipsaw* is a stock market term for a *fake-out*. Fortunately, there have not been a significant number of them.

I had now found a simple strategy for switching between large stocks and small stocks that gave me the superior returns of small stocks with reduced risk as measured by standard deviation. The good news was that the risk–return (Sharpe) ratio was also substantially higher than that of both small stocks and large stocks. This strategy also beat or matched large stocks for every decade except the 1930s. In the 1930s, the degree of underperformance was minimal, slightly less than 1 percent.

Summary

Many things influence the returns of small stocks, but the availability of money and credit is the primary factor in their long-term outperformance. In the world today, the U.S. Federal Reserve is the primary institution that drives this availability. The Follow the Fed Standard Strategy is based in large part on the following precepts:

- Buy small stocks when the real rate of interest is negative.
- Buy large stocks when it is not.

Looking for further insight into the Follow the Fed strategy? Visit www.FollowtheFedtheBook.com.

11

Follow the Fed: The Easy Strategy for True Wealth™ Step-By-Step Instructions

IMPLEMENTING THE STANDARD STRATEGY IN YOUR OWN PORTFOLIO

Implementing the Follow the Fed Standard Strategy in your portfolio is a relatively easy task. All you have to do is carry out the six steps covered in this chapter.

Step 1: Decide How Much to Invest

Although all the Follow the Fed strategies are tested using a $10,000 initial investment, the amount of money you choose to invest could be different (more or less) depending on your personal financial situation. The amount you choose to invest should fit into your long-term financial goals as determined by you and your financial advisor, if you have one.

If you use an investment advisor, make sure he or she understands that you will invest this portion of your portfolio in U.S. stocks using the Follow the Fed strategy—that is, switching between large stocks and small stocks from time to time. Once your advisor understands how the Follow the Fed Standard Strategy operates, he or she can help you determine the proper amount to allocate based on factors like your age, risk tolerance, and overall investment goals.

Step 2: Open an Investment Account

If you do not already have one, open an account with a low-cost brokerage service or mutual fund group. Investment services and the costs of those services can vary greatly across firms so it is worthwhile spending time researching your options before making a decision.

At the very least, start by assessing your current and near-future financial needs. Make a list of the products (stocks, bonds, etc.) you plan to manage in your account and decide how often you will trade. Wherever possible, estimate the amount of money you will be investing and the number of trades you will make on an annual basis. When researching brokerage firms, calculate your expected annual costs, as well as extra or hidden fees.

Some institutions charge a fee for each transaction, or you may have to pay a penalty if your account is inactive for a period. For most *buy and hold* investors, this is a fee to avoid.

Your decision will likely be based on a number of factors, such as cost, convenience, and range of services. Analyzing expected costs beforehand will help you narrow your choices.

When applying the Follow the Fed Standard Strategy to the period between 1928 and 2006, there were approximately 35 switches. This averages to a single switch approximately every 2.26 years. With so few transactions, the overall trading costs of applying the Standard Strategy should be relatively low through most brokerage/mutual fund groups.

Because the Follow the Fed Standard Strategy invests in baskets of large stocks and small stocks, you will want to be sensitive to the costs of buying and selling both domestic mutual funds and exchange traded funds (ETFs). These are the two primary investment products used in applying the Standard Strategy. Fortunately, these products are the building blocks of most portfolios and are accessible for buying and selling through most firms for a reasonable fee.

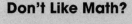

Don't Like Math?

Although the formula used to implement the Follow the Fed strategy is not difficult, some people just do not like doing any math at all! For those of you who would rather have someone else do it for you, please visit www.FollowtheFedtheBook.com.
For a nominal fee, we take care of all of the calculations and notify you when it is time to make a trade.

Step 3: Start a Follow the Fed Standard Strategy Notebook

Once you have determined how much money to invest and which investment service to use, your next step is to keep track of your purchases. You will only need to enter all of the historical data once, after which you will update it once a month.

(NOTE: For those of you who prefer using Microsoft Excel or another spreadsheet program to do these calculations,

Table 11.1   Follow the Fed Standard Strategy Grid

Date	T-Bill	T-Bill – 12m	Inflation	Inflation – 12m	Large/Small

please visit www.FollowtheFedtheBook.com for the formulas. Channel Capital Research Institute, LLC also offers a service to keep track of these data for you for a fee and even recommends low-cost ETFs and index funds.)

In your notebook, draw a table with labels, as in Table 11.1.

Step 4: Complete the Notebook

NOTE: Channel Capital Research Institute, LLC has used complex methodologies for calculating past performance numbers for both the 30-day Treasury bill (total return) and the consumer price index (CPI) total return. Although these methods lead to very accurate results, they may go beyond the needs of the individual investor. The good news is that most of the information you will need to complete the notebook is publicly available, and the calculations for completing the notebook can be simplified. Your numbers may not match our numbers exactly, but you should be able to get similar results that allow you to update your notebook on a monthly basis.

Date

For the purposes of this exercise, let us assume that the current date is March 1929. The month and year to which the historical data apply will be written in the first row (January 1928), starting with 15 months ago, and working down to the current month (March 1929). Your table should look like Table 11.2.

Table 11.2 Follow the Fed Standard Strategy Grid with Dates

Date	T-Bill	T-Bill – 12m	Inflation	Inflation – 12m	Large/Small
Jan 1928					
Feb 1928					
Mar 1928					
Apr 1928					
May 1928					
Jun 1928					
Jul 1928					
Aug 1928					
Sep 1928					
Oct 1928					
Nov 1928					
Dec 1928					
Jan 1929					
Feb 1929					
Mar 1929					

T-Bill

In this column, you will record the current one-month return on the U.S. government-issued 30-day Treasury bill. Government bond yield information is available in most newspapers (such as the *Wall Street Journal* or the *Financial Times*), or online on Web sites such as finance.yahoo.com or federalreserve.gov. Please visit www.FollowtheFedtheBook.com for additional links and resources.

Although the T-bill is often referred to as the 30-day T-bill by the media, the U.S. government actually auctions these bills with a 28-day (or four-week) maturity. As a result, the financial papers will often quote an annualized discount rate under the heading of either "28-day" or "4 weeks." Be aware that you will most likely be quoted an *annualized* rate. This annualized number will need to be converted to a monthly return.

It takes a bond analyst several complicated calculations to convert this annualized rate to a monthly return. We can avoid these calculations, however, by using an approximation for the monthly return: Divide the annualized rate you obtained from the newspaper by 12 (or 12 months). Although this method will not provide you with numbers that match our numbers exactly, it should give you a close enough approximation to be useful in your notebook.

For example, you find the "4-week Treasury bill auction" rate of 4.293 (or 4.293%) listed for the end of January 1928. You see that this number is annualized and in percentage (%) form, so you simply divide it by 1,200 (4.293/1200) to get an approximate monthly return in decimal form of 0.0036. Write this number in your notebook. You should make it a routine to try to update your notebook this way consistently at the beginning or end of each month, so that you have approximately 30 days between each of your recordings from the newspaper or the Web.

You can find the performance of the 30-day Treasury bills on the Internet and in print at the following sources:

- **Newspaper:** The *Wall Street Journal,* Money & Investing, Borrowing Benchmarks, U.S. government rates, Treasury bill auction (4 weeks)
- **Internet:** wsj.com, Markets, Market Data Center, Bonds/Rates/Credit Markets, Treasury Quotes, Bills (28 Days to Maturity)

As you fill in your monthly returns, your table should now look similar to Table 11.3. **(Please note the data presented are for demonstration purposes only.)**

Table 11.3   Follow the Fed Grid with Partial T-Bill Data

Date	T-Bill	T-Bill – 12m	Inflation	Inflation – 12m	Large/Small
Jan 1928	0.0036				
Feb 1928	0.0043				
Mar 1928	0.0040				
Apr 1928	0.0033				
May 1928	0.0043				

Date	T-Bill	T-Bill – 12m	Inflation	Inflation – 12m	Large/Small
Jun 1928	0.0042				
Jul 1928	0.0043				
Aug 1928	0.0043				
Sep 1928	0.0037				
Oct 1928	0.0051				
Nov 1928	0.0049				
Dec 1928	0.0016				
Jan 1929					
Feb 1929					
Mar 1929					

Treasury Bill–12m

In this column, you will calculate and record the trailing 12-month compound return using the last twelve monthly "T-bill" values from the table. Here is the general formula:

$$\text{T-bill} - 12\text{m} = (1 + \text{T-bill}_{month1}) \times (1 + \text{T-bill}_{month2})$$
$$\times (1 + \text{T-bill}_{month3}) \times (1 + \text{T-bill}_{month4})$$
$$\times (1 + \text{T-bill}_{month5}) \times (1 + \text{T-bill}_{month6})$$
$$\times (1 + \text{T-bill}_{month7}) \times (1 + \text{T-bill}_{month8})$$
$$\times (1 + \text{T-bill}_{month9}) \times (1 + \text{T-bill}_{month10})$$
$$\times (1 + \text{T-bill}_{month11}) \times (1 + \text{T-bill}_{month12}) - 1$$

Now we can plug in the numbers from the table. Let us start with January 1928 as the first month. The value for T-bill$_{month1}$ is 0.0036, and the formula for that portion of the equation looks like this:

$$\text{T-bill} - 12\text{m} = (1 + 0.0036), \text{ or T-bill} - 12\text{m} = (1.0036)$$

In February 1928, the value of T-bill$_{month2}$, which is 0.0043. The formula for the two months now is:

$$\text{T-bill} - 12\text{m} = (1.0036) \times (1.0043)$$

When the T-bill values for the third month, March 1928 through the twelfth month, December 1928 are placed in the equation, it reads like this:

$$
\begin{aligned}
\text{T-bill} - 12\text{m} = \; & (1.0036) \times (1.0043) \\
& \times (1.0040) \times (1.0033) \times (1.0043) \\
& \times (1.0042) \times (1.0043) \times (1.0043) \\
& \times (1.0037) \times (1.0051) \times (1.0049) \\
& \times (1.0016) - 1
\end{aligned}
$$

After completing the arithmetic, the equation results in T-bill $-$ 12m = 0.0486. Place this result (0.0486) in the T-bill $-$ 12m column and December 1928 row, as demonstrated in Table 11.4.

Because you will be completing these calculations on a monthly basis, let us do the next step and complete the calculations through January 1929. You have already completed the 12-month calculations for January to December

Table 11.4　Follow the Fed Grid Including T-Bill–12m Calculation

Date	T-Bill	T-Bill – 12m	Inflation	Inflation – 12m	Large/Small
Jan 1928	0.0036				
Feb 1928	0.0043				
Mar 1928	0.0040				
Apr 1928	0.0033				
May 1928	0.0043				
Jun 1928	0.0042				
Jul 1928	0.0043				
Aug 1928	0.0043				
Sep 1928	0.0037				
Oct 1928	0.0051				
Nov 1928	0.0049				
Dec 1928	0.0016	0.0486			
Jan 1929	0.0045				
Feb 1929					
Mar 1929					

1928, and now you need to complete the 12-month calculations for February 1928 to January 1929. Next, you need to complete the 12-month calculations for March 1928 to February 1929, and so on.

Let us complete the calculations for February 1928 to January 1929. You have already added the January 1929 T-bill value from the newspaper into the table (0.0045). Use the same T-bill − 12m general formula previously shown and plug in the correct values from the table into the formula. The value for the T-bill$_{month1}$ is now February 1928 (0.0043). The value for the T-bill$_{month2}$ is now March 1928 (0.0040). Continue down the table for each T-bill month all the way through January 1929, which is the value for T-bill$_{month12}$ (0.0045).

The sample equation for T-bill − 12m starting with February 1928 as the first month will look like this:

$$
\begin{aligned}
\text{T-bill} - 12\text{m} = {} & (1.0043) \times (1.0040) \times (1.0033) \\
& \times (1.0043) \times (1.0042) \times (1.0043) \\
& \times (1.0043) \times (1.0037) \times (1.0051) \\
& \times (1.0049) \times (1.0016) \times (1.0045) - 1
\end{aligned}
$$

After completing the arithmetic, the equation results for the second month of calculating the T-bill − 12m rate beginning with February 1928 and ending with January 1929, will be 0.0495. This result will now be placed in the T-bill −12m column and January 1929 row, as shown in Table 11.5.

Inflation

Now you are ready to begin the next column, which involves calculating inflation index changes from month to month.

Every month you need to record in your table the monthly change in inflation as indicated by the change in the CPI-U. This is an inflation index calculated by the government each month. Specifically, you will be calculating the *change* in the consumer price index (CPI) for *all urban consumers* (CPI-U)—*all items*; not seasonally adjusted, each

Table 11.5 Follow the Fed Grid with Second T-Bill–12m Calculation

Date	T-Bill	T-Bill – 12m	Inflation	Inflation –12m	Large/Small
Jan 1928	0.0036				
Feb 1928	0.0043				
Mar 1928	0.0040				
Apr 1928	0.0033				
May 1928	0.0043				
Jun 1928	0.0042				
Jul 1928	0.0043				
Aug 1928	0.0043				
Sep 1928	0.0037				
Oct 1928	0.0051				
Nov 1928	0.0049				
Dec 1928	0.0016	0.0486			
Jan 1929	0.0045	0.0495			
Feb 1929					
Mar 1929					

month. CPI-U information is available in most newspapers (including the *Wall Street Journal*), or online at any number of Web sites (*Yahoo! Finance,* and the *U.S. Department of Labor Bureau of Labor Statistics*).

For this calculation, you will work with the *actual* index value in order to calculate the monthly change. Use the following equation:

$$\text{Inflation} = \frac{(\text{This month's index value} - \text{Last month's index value})}{(\text{Last month's index value})}$$

(Please note the data presented are for demonstration purposes only.)

For example, you open your financial news source and see the CPI-U index value for the end of December 1927 is 17.300. You also note the index value of 17.300 for the end of January 1928. You find the index readings listed under *Consumer Price Index—All Items.* Assume that January 1928 is the current month. Now, calculate the inflation value for your notebook using our equation and write this number in your table. For example,

Inflation = (January 1928 index value − December 1927 index value)/(December 1927 index value)

When the December and January values are plugged into the equation, it should look like this:

Inflation = (17.300 − 17.300)/(17.300)
= (0.000)/(17.300) = 0.0000

Record this inflation value in the table for January 1928. Note that this inflation value can be *positive* or *negative,* depending on how the underlying CPI-U index value changes from month to month.

As I write, U.S. Department of Labor Bureau of Labor Statistics CPI-U data are available on the Internet and in print at the following sources:

- **Newspaper:** The *Wall Street Journal,* Money & Investing, Borrowing Benchmarks, Inflation, U.S. Consumer Price Index, Index Level (All Items)
- **Internet:** online.barrons.com, Market Lab, Economy & Money—Pulse of the Economy, Inflation, Consumer price index B (unadjusted)

As you fill in your monthly inflation numbers (as a decimal, not a percentage), your table should now look like Table 11.6.

Do this calculation each month and record it in your notebook or table in the row for the current month in the Inflation column. For example, you are placing it in the December 1928 row because you have just calculated the change in inflation between the months of November 1928 and December 1928.

Table 11.6   Follow the Fed Grid with Inflation Data

Date	T-Bill	T-Bill – 12m	Inflation	Inflation –12m	Large/Small
Jan 1928	0.0036		0.0000		
Feb 1928	0.0043		–0.0116		
Mar 1928	0.0040		0.0000		
Apr 1928	0.0033		0.0000		
May 1928	0.0043		0.0058		
Jun 1928	0.0042		–0.0058		
Jul 1928	0.0043		0.0000		
Aug 1928	0.0043		0.0000		
Sep 1928	0.0037		0.0117		
Oct 1928	0.0051		–0.0058		
Nov 1928	0.0049		0.0000		
Dec 1928	0.0016	0.0486	–0.0058		
Jan 1929	0.0045	0.0495	0.0000		
Feb 1929					
Mar 1929					

Inflation - 12m

Similar to the type of monthly calculation you did to determine the 12-month T-bill rate, now calculate the value for Inflation – 12m. This will show the *trailing 12-month compound return* using the last 12-month inflation values from the table. The general equation for this calculation is as follows:

$$
\begin{aligned}
\text{Inflation} - 12\text{m} \\
= (1 + \text{Inflation}_{month1}) \\
\times (1 + \text{Inflation}_{month2}) \times (1 + \text{Inflation}_{month3}) \\
\times (1 + \text{Inflation}_{month4}) \times (1 + \text{Inflation}_{month5}) \\
\times (1 + \text{Inflation}_{month6}) \times (1 + \text{Inflation}_{month7}) \\
\times (1 + \text{Inflation}_{month8}) \times (1 + \text{Inflation}_{month9}) \\
\times (1 + \text{Inflation}_{month10}) \times (1 + \text{Inflation}_{month11}) \\
\times (1 + \text{Inflation}_{month12}) - 1
\end{aligned}
$$

Once again, assume it is December 1928 and you are calculating the Inflation – 12m value for the months of

January 1928 to December 1928. The first month in the equation is January 1928 (0.0000) and the twelfth month is December 1928 (−0.0058). Complete the formula as before, filling in the appropriate numbers from the table. The equation should reads as follows:

$$
\begin{aligned}
\text{Inflation} - 12m = \;& (1.0000) \times (0.9884) \times (1.0000) \\
& \times (1.0000) \times (1.0058) \times (0.9942) \\
& \times (1.0000) \times (1.0000) \times (1.0117) \\
& \times (0.9942) \times (1.0000) \times (0.9942) \\
& - 1
\end{aligned}
$$

After completing the arithmetic, the equation results in Inflation − 12m = −0.0116. Place this result, −0.0116, in the Inflation − 12m column and December 1928 row.

As a second example, the following month, you will need to calculate the Inflation − 12m value using February 1928 as the first month, and January 1929 as the twelfth month. The equation and its result would read as follows:

$$
\begin{aligned}
\text{Inflation change} - 12m \\
= \;& (0.9884) \times (1.0000) \\
& \times (1.0000) \times (1.0058) \times (0.9942) \\
& \times (1.0000) \times (1.0000) \times (1.0117) \\
& \times (0.9942) \times (1.0000) \times (0.9942) \\
& \times (1.0000) - 1
\end{aligned}
$$

Inflation − 12m = −0.0116, rounded to the fourth decimal place. This value is now placed in the Inflation − 12m column and January 1929 row, as you can see in Table 11.7.

Large or Small (Stocks)

Now that the table is populated with Treasury and inflation data, we can use it to determine whether we should be invested in large or small stocks (final column). Due to an inherent time lag built into the government's inflation calculations, and the frequent revisions of the Inflation index (listed in the financial literature as CPI-U), Channel

Table 11.7   Follow the Fed Grid with Inflation – 12m Data

Date	T-Bill	T-Bill – 12m	Inflation	Inflation – 12m	Large/Small
Jan 1928	0.0036		0.0000		
Feb 1928	0.0043		–0.0116		
Mar 1928	0.0040		0.0000		
Apr 1928	0.0033		0.0000		
May 1928	0.0043		0.0058		
Jun 1928	0.0042		–0.0058		
Jul 1928	0.0043		0.0000		
Aug 1928	0.0043		0.0000		
Sep 1928	0.0037		0.0117		
Oct 1928	0.0051		–0.0058		
Nov 1928	0.0049		0.0000		
Dec 1928	0.0016	0.0486	–0.0058	–0.0116	
Jan 1929	0.0045	0.0495	0.0000	–0.0116	
Feb 1929					
Mar 1929					

Capital Research Institute, LLC uses a two-month time lag in determining the large/small signal. For example, at the end of January 1929, check to see if the December 1928 inflation index has been changed. If it has, change the Inflation number in the December 1928 row and recalculate the Inflation – 12m number in that row.

Refer to the sample Follow the Fed Standard Strategy (Table 11.7). Specifically, the March 1929 large/small stocks signal uses the data calculated in December 1928 to determine whether the signal for March 1929 is large or small for stocks. More specifically, the December 1928 T-bill – 12m value is compared to the December 1928 Inflation – 12m value in order to determine the large/small stock signal for March 1929.

Here is the comparison you will need to do: If the T-bill – 12m value for a given month is less than the Inflation – 12m value for that same month, then you enter "Small" in the Large/Small column two months ahead. If the T-bill – 12m

Table 11.8   Follow the Fed Grid with Large/Small Stock Notations

Date	T-Bill	T-Bill – 12m	Inflation	Inflation –12m	Large/Small
Jan 1928	0.0036		0.0000		
Feb 1928	0.0043		–0.0116		
Mar 1928	0.0040		0.0000		
Apr 1928	0.0033		0.0000		
May 1928	0.0043		0.0058		
Jun 1928	0.0042		–0.0058		
Jul 1928	0.0043		0.0000		
Aug 1928	0.0043		0.0000		
Sep 1928	0.0037		0.0117		
Oct 1928	0.0051		–0.0058		
Nov 1928	0.0049		0.0000		
Dec 1928	0.0016	0.0486	–0.0058	–0.0116	
Jan 1929	0.0045	0.0495	0.000	–0.0116	
Feb 1929					
Mar 1929					Large
Apr 1929					Large

value is greater than or equal to the Inflation – 12m value for the same month, then enter "Large" in the Large/Small column two months ahead.

For example, if the December 1928 T-bill – 12m value is 0.0486 and the December 1928 Inflation – 12m value is –0.0116, the signal for March 1929 is "Large." From December 1928, you will skip two months to allow for the government to revise its figures, and apply the December 1928 data to your March 1929 decisions regarding large or small stocks.

As the second example, let us look at the values for January 1929. During this month, the T-bill − 12m value was 0.0495 and the Inflation − 12m was –0.0116. Again we see that the T-bill − 12m value was larger than the Inflation − 12m value and we enter "Large" in the Large/Small column, skipping two months ahead to April 1929, as seen in Table 11.8.

Step 5: Determine What You Will Buy —Mutual Funds or Exchange Traded Funds (ETFs)

Now that you have determined to buy large or small stocks, you must decide how to make these different baskets of stocks available for your personal investment portfolio. Typically, this is done through stock mutual funds, stock index funds, or stock-based exchange traded funds (ETFs).

If the results of your calculations indicated large stocks, look for an investment that closely tracks the performance of large stocks. Similarly, if the results of your calculations indicated small stocks, look for an investment that closely tracks the performance of small stocks.

Because expense ratios and portfolio compositions can vary greatly from fund to fund, you may wish to discuss your available investment options with your financial advisor, or visit www.FollowtheFedtheBook.com for additional resources. You should be able to determine a suitable investment option for each of the signals generated by the Follow the Fed Standard Strategy.

Step 6: Buy and Wait for the Next Large/Small Signal

Knowing the large/small signal based on the results of your calculations, you are now ready to invest. Use your brokerage account to purchase mutual fund shares or ETF shares and then . . . relax!

Check the Follow the Fed Standard Strategy signal each month to see if it has changed. If it has not changed, you do nothing. If it has changed, you will need to switch your investment to the appropriate fund.

If you do not want to track the large/small stock signals yourself, the Channel Capital Research Institute, LLC, provides services to track the signals for you for a small fee. If you are interested in these and other services, please go to www.FollowtheFedtheBook.com for additional information.

Summary

I have reviewed the six steps involved in applying Follow the Fed to your own investment portfolio. The initial step is to decide how much money you are going to invest, and the second is to open an investment account.

Steps 3 and 4 involve the creation and completion of your Follow the Fed notebook. The process of doing so is detailed in Step 4.

Step 5 involves decision making, based on the data you have developed in Step 4. This is where you choose the mutual funds or ETFs for your portfolio.

Step 6 monitors the Follow the Fed signal once a month. If there has been no change, then do nothing. However, if the signal has changed, then it is time to switch your investment to the appropriate fund.

For downloadable Follow the Fed worksheets visit the Web site www.FollowtheFedtheBook.com.

12

How to Use Follow the Fed for All Types of Investments

I have taken you through the development of my Follow the Fed Standard Strategy. You now understand the history that stands behind the strategy from the robber barons of the 1800s to the creation of the U.S. Federal Reserve in the early 1900s. You can see how the massive power of the Fed controls the availability of money and credit in the United States, as well as on a global basis. (If you wish to read more on the Federal Reserve System, see the Appendix.)

You now also understand how the Fed affects the performance of small stocks and large stocks and how to use this relationship to allocate your investment capital between the two categories. This understanding will allow you to manage your equity investments, either by yourself or through an advisor, with the potential to outperform most investment professionals.

The greatest benefit of the Follow the Fed Standard Strategy is that it is a simple, low-cost investing strategy requiring minimal time and effort on your part.

Remember the hassles associated with an active trading system? If you work during the day, your boss could find you focusing on the market instead of your job. If you are on vacation, you need to have your laptop with you. Your mind will be everywhere but the trip, ruining it for everyone. If you are retired you stay glued to your computer, ignoring your family and friends. As you can see, trading can cause lots of stress and tension in your life. With the Follow the Fed Standard Strategy, you will not have these problems.

You are now in control of your investment destiny because now you understand how Wall Street operates. It is not some black hole in space into which your money disappears, while you hope and pray that it comes back. You now have a logical framework to understand what is going on, and you can make your own decisions. Even if you choose to work with an advisor, you are still in control. Knowledge *is* Power.

Let us look at how the Follow the Fed Standard Strategy can be used with a variety of investment vehicles.

Mutual Funds

I address mutual funds first because most investors use them. There are many mutual funds that fit into the categories of large stocks and small stocks. The mutual fund group you already own probably has products that will do nicely.

If you currently have a mutual fund but you are not sure what type it is, you can do any one of the following:

- Go to http://finance.yahoo.com and enter your mutual fund name.
- Check the prospectus that came with your mutual fund.
- Call your broker, or the management company that invests the fund.

You know my preference is for low-cost index funds for the reasons mentioned earlier in this book. However, if you decide to venture outside the index fund arena, I have one piece of advice. *Watch the fees!*

There are two types of mutual fund fees and expenses: the *one-time fees* and the *ongoing fees*.

The one-time fees fall into one of the following categories:

- **Sales fees:** These are often referred to as *sales load* and may be charged when you enter the fund (front-end) *and* when you exit it (back-end). They are usually paid to the mutual fund company, the broker, or salesperson.
- **Redemption fees:** These usually refer to fees charged for early redemption in order to discourage short-term trading and "market timing." These fees are not bad for the long-term investor as long as they are reinvested into the fund and not pocketed by the fund managers, brokers, or salespersons.

The ongoing fees are charged every year and impact the performance of the fund, even for the long-term investor:

- **Expense ratio:** This is the total of the annual expenses of the fund, expressed as a percentage of assets in the fund. It includes the management fee paid to the mutual fund manager, operating and administrative fees paid to run the fund, and 12b-1 fees used to market and to distribute the fund.
- **Brokerage costs:** These are costs to the fund for buying and selling securities. Often, this information is not readily available and can be found only in the prospectus.

I strongly urge you to avoid sales fees for several reasons:

- When a sale commission is charged, you must outperform a similar fund without a commission by that amount just to match its performance.
- A sales load locks you into the fund. You need to stay in it for a long time to cover this cost and still get a competitive rate of return.
- These load funds rarely justify the sales commission in comparison to no-load funds, unless the advisor is

using this to compensate for other benefits, such as financial planning, that are being provided. My preference is that he or she charges separately for these activities. This arrangement avoids the problems just mentioned.

Exchange Traded Funds (ETFs)

Exchange traded funds (ETFs) are similar to mutual funds because they usually represent an ownership interest in a portfolio of securities. However, they can be bought or sold like a stock, usually on a major stock exchange. ETFs can also have certain tax advantages for the long-term holder.

There has been an incredible increase in the use and popularity of ETFs in the market. There has also been an increase in the number and types of ETFs. Remember first to determine the category of your ETF (large stocks or small stocks).

These are some of the issues you should consider when choosing an Exchange Traded Fund:

- Keep it simple. Remember Occam's Razor. There are ETFs now proliferating in every shape and flavor. Some are quite complicated. In general, stick to the plain vanilla ones.
- Liquidity is crucial. Be certain that your ETF has sufficient liquidity to buy and to sell when you want. This is one reason that I like older, more established ETFs.
- As with mutual funds, low fees are extremely important.

401(k) and Retirement Plans (including 403B and 529)

My Follow the Fed strategy works very well with 401(k) and retirement plans. These plans usually offer you a fixed menu of choices with no substitutions allowed. Therefore, other investment strategies that require investment into specific stocks or mutual funds may not work.

Since Follow the Fed applies only to stock *categories,* it is much easier to use. Most 401(k) and retirement plans have at least one choice that qualifies as either large stocks or small stocks. You can usually determine this by examining the plan's literature or asking the plan administrator.

Dealing with Your Financial Advisor

Your financial advisor may notice a big difference in dealing with you after you have read this book. You will probably be more confident and will have a better understanding of what he or she is saying. You are now taking control of your portfolio. Your advisor may recommend other forms of asset allocation with your portfolio and may even be uncomfortable with Follow the Fed. As I mentioned, it is fine to start with a small portion of your portfolio until you are comfortable with the methodology. Remember that this is *your* money!

I have noticed that the best financial advisors are open to new ideas and information. They sincerely want to do the right thing for their clients. Also, they can perform valuable financial planning services, like Ms. Advisor did for Joe Investor in Chapter 1.

For Stockpickers Only

This section is for investors who want to invest in individual stocks or to do so through a managed account program, mutual fund, or hedge fund.

I never said that there were not superior stockpickers. There are definitely superstars out there. Warren Buffett and Jeff Vinik are great examples of that breed. I simply said that superior stockpicking is an incredibly difficult task. The odds are against the average investor being successful at it. Finding someone to manage his or her money, who has incredible insight, superior connections, and great luck is difficult.

If you feel that you are among the elite few, the Follow the Fed strategies can still benefit even the most diehard stockpicker. The odds of picking the right stocks are better if you are in the right stock type. The Fama–French research that was cited earlier demonstrates that the stock type is more important than the actual stock itself. Remember my earlier comparison in Chapter 7 to housing: *"It's not the House; it's the Neighborhood."*

Remember the late 1990s. If you were in any large, growth stocks, your odds of superior returns were much higher than if you were in small, value stocks. So, if you decide to try your luck at picking individual stocks, use Follow the Fed to get you into the right neighborhood.

For Traders Only

Trading is an even more difficult game than stockpicking. With trading, your timing and execution generally have to be perfect. If you are late, your profit can disappear in a flash. Brokerage fees, commissions, slippage, and sometimes leverage are also much higher. Often, traders lose small amounts frequently but make almost all their profits in a few trades. This takes tremendous discipline and lots of time and can be extremely painful for the average person. In my opinion, the odds are stacked against being successful in trading.

However, there are superior traders out there, such as Stevie Cohen and Jim Simons, whom I mentioned in earlier chapters. If you feel that you are an incredible trader or know one, you can still benefit from Follow the Fed for the reasons mentioned above for stockpickers. Integrate it into your trading plan.

Get Started!

The hardest part of any journey in life is said to be the first step. If you do not take it, nothing ever happens. Now that you have the knowledge and the power, you must begin to apply the Follow the Fed Standard Strategy in your investment portfolio. You do not have to do it all at once. Start with a small portion of your investable capital. As you become more comfortable and confident, you can apply the strategy to other parts of your portfolio.

Summary

In this chapter I looked at how the Follow the Fed Standard Strategy can be used with a variety of investment vehicles, including mutual funds, exchange traded funds (ETFs), and 401(k) and retirement funds. I also shared my thoughts on working with your financial advisor, if you have one. Remember, it is your money, and the best advisors are those who are open to additional ideas and information.

The important points from this chapter are as follows:

- In general, keep your fees low when it comes to mutual funds and exchange traded funds (ETFs).
- The Follow the Fed Standard Strategy works well with 401(k) and retirement plans because its focus on types of stocks (large stocks or small stocks) can be adapted to the fixed menu of choices offered in these plans.
- Traders and stockpickers can benefit by being in the right types of stocks first.

The most important thing is perhaps the most difficult. It is getting started, taking that first step. Now that you have the knowledge and the power, you must begin to apply the Follow the Fed Standard Strategy in your investment portfolio. It is that simple.

For further details on applying the Follow the Fed strategy to your investment portfolio, visit www.Followthe FedtheBook.com.

CHAPTER

13

Advanced Follow the Fed Strategies

You now have a logical framework to understand the nature of stock investing and the tools to use the strategy by yourself or with your advisor. The Follow the Fed Standard Strategy has the potential to deliver long-term investment returns comparable to the top tier of Wall Street experts with minimal effort and expense on your part.

You may be thinking, "Is that it? Is there anything else? Is there a way to improve my returns even more?" The answer is *yes*. There are other Follow the Fed strategies that can potentially improve your long-term investment returns. Let's examine them in more detail.

Follow the Fed Filtered Strategy

The biggest challenge with the Follow the Fed Standard Strategy is whipsaws. As I discussed in Chapter 10, these are situations in which the Standard Follow the Fed Strategy generates a signal and then quickly reverses itself, possibly generating a loss because of trading costs or taxes. In addition to the transaction costs involved, whipsaws can involve a substantial amount of emotional stress and pain. This is something that we want to minimize to the greatest extent possible.

Channel Capital Research Institute, LLC has developed a proprietary filter to attempt to reduce the number of whip-saws and thus the number of trades and to increase returns. The Follow the Fed Filtered Strategy increases the return from 1928 to 2006 from 12.85 percent to 12.96 percent and reduces the number of trades from 35 to 21. It also increases the average time between trades from 2.26 years to 3.76 years.

This may not seem like a massive improvement. However, $10,000 invested in the Filtered version during this period would become $151,332,866 compared to $140,098,806, had you invested in the Standard version without deducting for any trading costs. See Figure 13.1 and Table 13.1 for full details.

Although risk as measured by standard deviation increased slightly, the return rate also increased slightly. Therefore, the risk–return (Sharpe) ratio remained about the same, with 40 percent fewer trades. You can read more about this on my Web site, www.FollowtheFedtheBook.com.

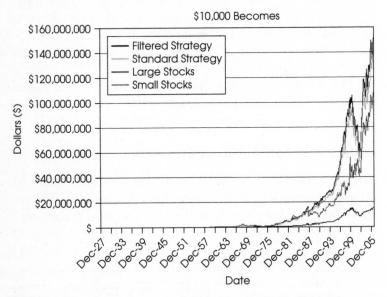

Figure 13.1   Performance of Follow the Fed Filtered and Standard Strategies, Large Stocks and Small Stocks (1928 to 2006)

Table 13.1   Summary Return Results for Follow the Fed Strategies: Large and Small Stocks (1928 to 2006)

	Filtered Strategy	Standard Strategy	Large Stocks[3]	Small Stocks[4]
Compound annual return	12.96%	12.85%	9.76%	12.47%
Risk (standard deviation of return)	0.2878	0.2848	0.1918	0.3722
Return–risk (Sharpe) ratio	0.4417	0.4403	0.4032	0.3887
Number of trades	21	35	–	–
Compound Annual Return by Decade				
1920s[1]	12.01%	12.01%	12.01%	−11.20%
1930s	−1.24%	−1.24%	−0.29%	2.94%
1940s	18.97%	18.97%	8.75%	19.91%
1950s	18.81%	18.58%	18.20%	19.04%
1960s	7.35%	7.35%	7.35%	15.38%
1970s	15.77%	14.92%	5.88%	8.77%
1980s	19.85%	19.48%	17.55%	12.11%
1990s	18.21%	18.44%	18.21%	13.96%
2000s[2]	5.94%	6.38%	1.13%	14.55%
$10,000 becomes:	$151,332,866	$140,098,806	$15,675,227	$107,597,565
Correlation to large stocks	0.8856	0.8858	1.0000	0.7789

Source: Data drawn from the Kenneth R. French, Ph.D., Data Library (http://mba. tuck.dartmouth.edu/pages/faculty/ken.french/index.html), and Standard and Poor's (www.standardandpoors.com). Data current as of September 25, 2007. Actual live signals issued from ChannelCapitalResearch.com were used for 2006.

Total holding period: January 1, 1928, to December 31, 2006.
[1]January 1, 1928, to December 31, 1929.
[2]January 1, 2000, to December 31, 2006.
[3]Large Stock Index: 1928–1969 (Kenneth R. French, Ph.D., Data Library: Size Portfolio, Value Weighted Returns, Hi 20, Total Return), 1970–2006, and Standard and Poor's S&P 500 Total Return.
[4]Small Stock Index: Kenneth R. French, Ph.D., Data Library: Size Portfolio, Value Weighted Returns, Lo 20, Total Return.

Follow the Fed Proprietary Strategy

In addition to real interest rates, there are other factors that affect the relationship between large stocks and small stocks. One of them is the perception of risk associated with them. When small stocks are perceived as riskier, investors tend to retreat to large stocks. However, when the risk level associated with small stocks decreases, investors often return to them. You see a similar relationship with credit spreads associated with higher-quality and lower-quality bonds.

The best example of this was the late 1990s. Investors favored large stocks, especially growth stocks in the technology sector. The opposite was true for small, value stocks. When this pattern reversed itself in 2000, small stocks did well for the most part even as large stocks entered a multi-year bear market.

The Follow the Fed Proprietary Strategy incorporates several of these relationships to develop superior long-term returns on both an absolute and risk-return basis switching between large stocks and small stocks. From 1928 to 2006, the proprietary strategy returned 15.51 percent, as opposed to 12.96 percent and 12.85 percent for the Filtered and Standard Strategies respectively. In addition, $10,000 invested in the Proprietary Strategy during this period would become $882,776,671, compared to $151,332,866 with the filtered strategy and $140,098,806 with the Standard Strategy without deducting for any trading costs. Only 26 trades would have been generated—a trade about every 3.0 years. See Figure 13.2 and Table 13.2.

Although the Proprietary Strategy has the highest returns and the highest risk–return ratio in the long term, there are times when it underperforms the Filtered and Standard Strategies, as it would have done in the 1970s and the 1980s. However, degree of underperformance during these decades ranged from only approximately 1.0 to 3.8 percent. For more information, please visit my Web site, www.FollowtheFedthe Book.com.

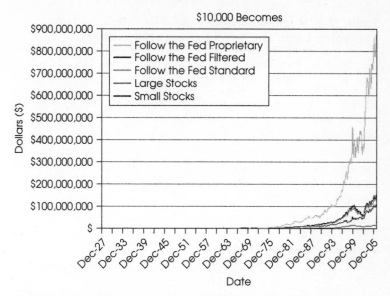

Figure 13.2 Performance of All Follow the Fed Strategies, Large Stocks and Small Stocks (1928 to 2006)

Twin Foundations™ Strategies

If we further divide our classification of stocks into growth and value as well as large-, mid-, and small-cap stocks, investment performance can be improved even more. In addition, we can try to minimize the impact of bear markets on an investment portfolio. You can read more about it online at www.FollowtheFedtheBook.com.

Summary

I proposed in Chapter 12 that the Follow the Fed Standard Strategy has the potential to deliver long-term investment returns comparable to the top tier of Wall Street experts with minimal effort and expense on your part. There are, however, two variations that will produce even greater returns on your investments.

The Follow the Fed Filtered Strategy increases the return from 1928 to 2006 to 12.96 percent from 12.85 percent

Table 13.2   Summary Return Results for Follow the Fed Strategies: Large and Small Stocks (1928 to 2006)

	Proprietary Strategy	Filtered Strategy	Standard Strategy	Large[3] S&P 500	Small[4]
Compound annual return	15.51%	12.96%	12.85%	9.76%	12.47%
Risk (standard deviation of return)	0.3314	0.2878	0.2848	0.1918	0.3722
Risk–return (Sharpe) ratio	0.4831	0.4417	0.4403	0.4032	0.3887
Number of trades	26	21	35	–	–
Compound Annual Return by Decade					
1920s[1]	12.01%	12.01%	12.01%	12.01%	–11.20%
1930s	4.45%	–1.24%	–1.24%	–0.29%	2.94%
1940s	21.73%	18.97%	18.97%	8.75%	19.91%
1950s	18.95%	18.81%	18.58%	18.20%	19.04%
1960s	15.51%	7.35%	7.35%	7.35%	15.38%
1970s	14.74%	15.77%	14.92%	5.88%	8.77%
1980s	16.02%	19.85%	19.48%	17.55%	12.11%
1990s	19.37%	18.21%	18.44%	18.21%	13.96%
2000s[2]	14.55%	5.94%	6.38%	1.13%	14.55%
$10,000 becomes:	$882,776,671	$151,332,866	$140,098,806	$15,675,227	$107,597,565
Correlation to Large Stocks	0.7904	0.8856	0.8858	1.0000	0.7789

Source: Data drawn from the Kenneth R. French, Ph.D., Data Library (http://mba. tuck.dartmouth.edu/pages/faculty/ken.french/index.html), and Standard and Poor's (www.standardandpoors.com). Data current as of September 25, 2007. Actual live signals issued from ChannelCapitalResearch.com were issued for 2006.

Total holding period: January 1, 1928, to December 31, 2006.
[1]January 1, 1928, to December 31, 1929.
[2]January 1, 2000, to December 31, 2006.
[3]Large Stock Index: 1928–1969 (Kenneth R. French, Ph.D., Data Library: Size Portfolio, Value Weighted Returns, Hi 20, Total Return), 1970–2006, and Standard and Poor's S&P 500 Total Return.
[4]Small Stock Index: Kenneth R. French, Ph.D., Data Library: Size Portfolio, Value Weighted Returns, Lo 20, Total Return.

and reduces the number of trades to 21 from 35. It also increases the average time between trades from 2.26 years to 3.76 years.

The Follow the Fed Proprietary Strategy incorporates several of the relationship factors between small and large stocks to develop superior long-term returns on both an absolute and risk-return basis, while switching between large and small stocks.

Additional information on these advanced Follow the Fed and Twin Foundations™ strategies can be found online at www.FollowtheFedtheBook.com.

CHAPTER 14

Conclusion

As you come to the end of this book, you need to remember that it is not the conclusion of your investing career. In fact for many of you, it may be just the beginning! In the same way that Joe Investor learned from his mistakes with Wall Street, I hope that you have been able to learn from the information I have offered in this book.

The saying, "Knowledge is Power" is truly applicable to successful investing. If you really understand what you are doing (or what is being done on your behalf), your odds of success greatly increase. Joe Investor's problems in Chapter 1 developed because he relied on emotion and instinct instead of his own intelligence. If you know the facts, think logically, and act as an educated consumer, you have a much better chance of beating the market and handling any problems that may arise.

At the end of this chapter, I recap my investing lessons that appear throughout the book. Use them as guidelines to assist you to navigate your way through the pitfalls of the Wall Street jungle. They offer common-sense advice that you might also pass along to a friend or loved one. They are designed to be an easy way to remember the important ideas you need to take with you when you decide to apply the Follow the Fed strategies.

In Chapters 3 and 4, I showed you that the power of banks to influence the availability of money and credit and its huge effect on the stock market is not some temporary, short-term phenomenon. This has been occurring over hundreds of years and is likely to continue in the future. The Federal Reserve is merely the latest and most powerful version of a banking powerhouse. Its form may change again in the future, but the principles will remain the same.

In Chapters 5 and 6, I introduced the investor's secret weapon: the power of compound interest in building true wealth over long periods of time. If you forget everything else from this book, please remember this principle. If you can lengthen your time frame, you will truly have an advantage over some of the giant Wall Street players who are locked into short-term performance. This is your Edge! Refer to Chapter 6 for the 10 essentials (plus 1).

In Chapters 7 and 8, I presented evidence that shows how difficult it is to beat the performance of large stocks. However, small stocks have a long history of being able to accomplish this at a price: short periods of massive outperformance accompanied by long periods of lagging large stocks.

In Chapters 9, 10, and 11, I demonstrated that the key to solving this dilemma is to understand why it occurs. After you gain this insight, you can use my strategy to profit from it. The great thing is that this strategy is easy to apply and does not take a tremendous amount of time. It increases your odds of long-term investing success while allowing you to enjoy life. What good is material wealth if we cannot use it to enjoy all the true riches that life has to offer? Remember to visit www. FollowtheFedtheBook.com if you want us to do the math for you and even tell you when to make the trades.

In Chapter 12, I showed how this strategy can be used with all your investments. This is especially true for 401(k) and other retirement plans, for which conventional investment advice is usually difficult to apply. This strategy is not some grand theory, but is instead a powerful tool that you can utilize to improve your investment returns.

In Chapter 13, I mentioned that the Follow the Fed Standard Strategy is simply the beginning. More advanced strategies of the Federal Reserve can increase your long-term returns even further. I have included additional information in the Appendix for those who want to learn in greater detail how the Fed operates. The Web site, www. FollowtheFedtheBook.com, has bonus material. Visit the site often for updates and news on Follow the Fed strategies.

However, you must remember that these are simply weapons in your investing arsenal. You have to be the one to make it happen. To be successful financially, you must be willing to make the commitments spelled out in the Introduction:

- I will think outside the box and rely on my own common sense.
- I will take charge of my own financial future.
- I will take action to make things happen.

The decision is in your hands!
I wish you the best of success in your investing career.

Douglas S. Roberts

The Follow the Fed Investment Lessons

Investment Lesson #1: Profitable investing is not like a contagious disease that you catch from being around the right people.

Investment Lesson #2: What makes Wall Street rich does not necessarily make the customers wealthy.

Investment Lesson #3: When it comes to investing, it is better to be smart than lucky! If you are smart, you make your own luck.

Investment Lesson #4: Think long term regarding both *return* and *risk* when analyzing your investments.

Investment Lesson #5: Outperforming the benchmark averages, such as the S&P 500, over the long term is much more difficult and rare than is commonly thought.

Investment Lesson #6: To be a successful investor you have to understand your strategy, to have complete confidence in it and to take responsibility for your investing decisions.

Investment Lesson #7: A successful investing strategy may be unconventional, controversial, and unpopular.

Investment Lesson #8: Successful investing involves making smart decisions and not necessarily working hard.

Investment Lesson #9: Do not let your ego prevent you from taking advantage of incredible investment opportunities.

Investment Lesson #10: Investing is like driving a car. Never do it with your eyes closed!

Investment Lesson #11: The golden rule of investing history is, "He who hath the gold maketh the rules."

Investment Lesson #12: The key to successful investing is to focus on your ultimate goal of getting wealthy (or wealthier).

Investment Lesson #13: Success with any investment strategy requires you, the investor, to understand it clearly and to have confidence in it.

Investment Lesson #14: Focus on achieving superior rates of return that are realistic, not just empty promises.

Investment Lesson #15: Any successful investment strategy will occasionally underperform, but it will work in the long run.

Investment Lesson #16: Your tolerance for risk must match that of your investment strategy in order to be successful.

Investment Lesson #17: Without the power of compounding, an investment strategy will not succeed.

Investment Lesson #18: Understanding who you are is perhaps the most important requirement for investment success.

Investment Lesson #19: Having a life outside investing will dramatically decrease the stress of sticking with your investment strategy.

Investment Lesson #20: Without self-control and commitment, successful investing is very difficult.

Investment Lesson #21: Action is required to make things happen in investing.

Investment Lesson #22: If you use a financial advisor, he or she must agree with your goals and philosophy and understand that you are in charge.

Remember to visit Follow the Fed on the Web for updates and additional resources: www.FollowtheFedtheBook.com.

Appendix: The Workings of the Federal Reserve System

This appendix is for those who have keener interest in how the Fed operates on a day-to-day basis. Chapter 4 covered the history of the Federal Reserve System, and now we will look at the finer points in the structure and machinations of the organization.

Much of the information here is summarized or taken directly from the government publication, *The Federal Reserve System: Purposes and Functions,* available from the Federal Reserve Web site, www.federalreserve.gov/.

Other sites that offer information on the Fed:

Federal Reserve Online: www.federalreserveonline.org/

Federal Reserve Education: www.federalreserveeducat ion.org/

The Federal Reserve System is the central bank of the United States. Created in 1913, it was designed to provide the nation with a *safe, flexible,* and *stable* monetary and financial system to replace the chaos of the previous decades. The economic disruptions of repeated bank failures and the business and personal bankruptcies that had plagued those earlier years were crippling the nation, and the new Federal Reserve System was to put an end to the economy's vulnerabilities.

The Federal Reserve System is an *independent* central bank, because its decisions do not have to be ratified by anyone in the executive branch of the government, including the president. It is the U.S. Congress that is responsible for overseeing the Fed.[1]

The Federal Reserve System has four major components:

1. Twelve individually chartered corporations are called Federal Reserve Banks.
2. Member commercial banks in each District contribute capital to the Reserve Banks and receive dividends.
3. The board of governors of the Federal Reserve System, a federal government agency, exercises general supervision over the Reserve Banks.
4. The Federal Open Market Committee (FOMC) is the main body for carrying out monetary policy.

We will examine each of these components in greater detail in the rest of this appendix. However, I recommend that you visit the Federal Reserve System Web site, where you can learn a great deal more than it is possible to include here.

The Goals and Overall Structure of the Fed

President Woodrow Wilson signed the Federal Reserve Act in 1913, marking the birth of the Fed. Over the years, successive legislative acts were ratified to better meet the objectives of economic growth, high employment, stable prices, and moderate long-term interest rates.[2]

The Federal Reserve System has these duties:

1. Conduct the nation's monetary policy.
2. Supervise and regulate banking institutions.
3. Maintain the stability of the financial system.
4. Provide financial services to depository banks, the U.S. government, and official foreign institutions.

The central structure of the Fed, the *board of governors*, oversees the 12 regional Federal Reserve Banks. The responsibilities of *supervision* and *regulation* of financial institutions are *shared* between the board of governors and the 12 regional member institutions.

There is also the Federal Open Market Committee, the FOMC, made up of the board of governors, the president of the Federal Reserve Bank of New York, and presidents of four other member Reserve Banks, who serve on a rotating basis. Overseeing *market operations* is the main tool used by the Fed to influence monetary and credit conditions.[3] This is the heart of the financial body known as the Federal Reserve System. We will examine the operation of the FOMC later; for now, let us continue with the structural elements.

The Board of Governors

The board consists of seven members who are appointed by the president of the United States and confirmed by the Senate.

The term of office is 14 years. There is an ingenious appointment schedule, to ensure *continuity* and *stability* within the board. These important aspects are secured by a staggering of the appointments to the board, one term expiring every two years.

Heading the board are the *chairman* and *vice chairman*, appointed by the U.S. president to serve four-year terms. It is the chairman of the board of governors who reports (twice a year) to Congress on the Fed's monetary policy objectives. He also testifies before Congress on other economic issues, and meets with the secretary of the treasury on a regular basis. The other six board members are routinely called to testify before Congress and must maintain regular contact with other government organizations as well.

One of the duties of a governor is to lead a committee—or committees—that study current economic issues. The board exercises broad supervisory control over *member banks*, as well as the companies that own the banks. This control is designed to ensure that each member bank operates in a responsible way, complying with federal regulations.

In addition, the board oversees the activities of the 12 Federal Reserve Banks, approving the appointments of the president of each institution, and three members of the Federal Reserve Banks' boards of directors. The most important thing they do, in relation to investors using the Follow the Fed strategy, is this: The seven governors, along with their economic analysts and support staff, *formulate the policies that affect the U.S. economy,* as part of the Federal Open Market Committee (FOMC).

The Network of Member Banks

The Federal Reserve System is made up of 12 Federal Reserve Districts, and a major city in each is home to a Federal Reserve Bank. Most of the Reserve Banks also have branch offices in their district; there are 25 of these branch offices throughout the nation. See Figure A.1.

Each of the 12 Federal Reserve Banks has a Web site, and most have fascinating archives of educational material. Here is a list of the Web sites for every regional Reserve Bank:

Atlanta, Georgia: www.frbatlanta.org/

Boston, Massachusetts: www.bos.frb.org/

Chicago, Illinois: www.chicagofed.org/

Cleveland, Ohio: www.clevelandfed.org/

Dallas, Texas: http://dallasfed.org/index.cfm

Kansas City, Missouri: www.kansascityfed.org/

Minneapolis, Minnesota: www.minneapolisfed.org/

New York, New York: www.newyorkfed.org/

Philadelphia, Pennsylvania: www.philadelphiafed.org/

Richmond, Virginia: www.richmondfed.org/

St. Louis, Missouri: http://stlouisfed.org/default.cfm

San Francisco, California: www.frbsf.org/

Each of the 12 Federal Reserve Banks is separately incorporated, and each has its own board of directors. The board appoints a president to serve a five-year term, subject to approval of the Federal Reserve System board of governors.

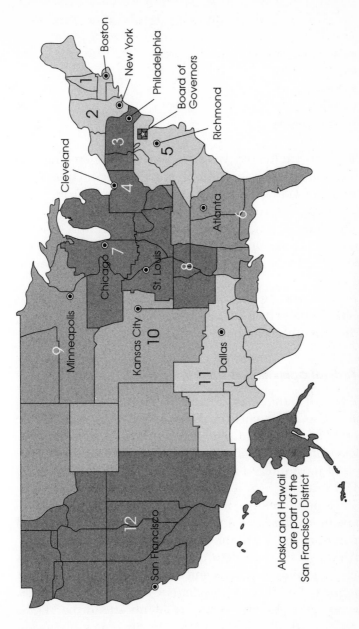

Figure A.1 U.S. Map with Federal Reserve Bank Locations

Source: *The Federal Reserve System Purposes and Functions* (www.federalreserve.gov).

The directors of each Reserve Bank board serve three-year terms and represent differing sectors of the economy:

- Business and industry
- Agriculture
- Finance
- Labor
- Consumers

The Federal Reserve Banks receive no budgeted monies from Congress; each is self-sufficient, earning income from interest on holdings of U.S. Treasury securities, from interest on loans, and from fees for services.

The stock of these Reserve Banks is owned entirely by the commercial banks that are members of the Federal Reserve System. Dividends are paid semiannually to shareholders at a *fixed* rate.

It is interesting to note that at the end of each year, Reserve Banks return *all earnings in excess of expenses* necessary for operations to the U.S. Treasury.

The Federal Open Market Committee (FOMC)

Here we are at the heart of the Fed. The structure I just discussed exists to support the decision-making process of the Federal Open Market Committee (FOMC), responsible for *the formulation and conduct of monetary policy.* It is the FOMC that is of most interest to investors working with the Follow the Fed strategy.

The committee is composed of 12 members. Membership includes all seven of the Federal Reserve System board of governors and *five* of the Reserve Bank presidents.

Although the president of the New York Reserve Bank serves on a *continuous* basis and is the vice chairman of the committee, the other 11 presidents serve on a rotating basis. However, *all* 12 Reserve Bank presidents attend the FOMC meetings, and all actively participate in policy discussion and analytical processes.

The FOMC meets *eight times* a year in Washington, D.C. Each meeting is structured in much the same way. A senior official of the Federal Reserve Bank of New York discusses developments in the financial and foreign exchange markets, as well as activities of the New York Fed's domestic and foreign trading desks (more about the *desks* later).

Staff members from the board of governors then present their financial forecasts. The dialogue widens as the board's governors and all 12 Reserve Bank presidents offer their personal views on the economic outlook.

In such an open forum, the FOMC discusses the options that would best promote the economy's *sustainable* growth. After all talk is done, members vote on a directive that is issued to the New York Fed's domestic trading desk. This directive informs the desk of the committee's objective for *open market operation*—whether to *ease, tighten,* or *maintain* the current FOMC policy.

Advisory Committees

The Federal Reserve System uses a number of advisory committees in its day-to-day operations. Three committees advise the board of governors directly:

The Federal Advisory Committee is composed of 12 representatives of the banking industry. It advises the board on *all* matters within the board's jurisdiction. It meets four times a year, as required by the Federal Reserve Act. Every year, each of the 12 member Reserve Banks chooses one person to represent its district on the Federal Advisory Committee, and those members customarily serve three one-year terms.

The Consumer Advisory Committee was established in 1976 to advise the board on issues relating to consumer financial services. Members are appointed by the board of governors and serve staggered three-year terms. The council meets three times a year in Washington, D.C., and the meetings are *open to the public.*

The Thrift Institutions Advisory Committee was established after the passage of the *Depository Institutions Deregulation and Monetary Control Act* of 1980, under President Carter. Its purpose is to obtain information and views on the special needs and problems of *thrift* institutions, which are depositories for consumer savings. The most common varieties are the *Savings and Loan Association* and the *Savings Bank.*

This committee provides advice from representatives of institutions that have an important relationship with the Federal Reserve. They meet with the board of governors in Washington, D.C., three times a year. Members are appointed by the board of governors and generally serve for two years.

The 12 Federal Reserve Banks also use advisory committees. The most important are the committees that advise the Bank on matters of agriculture, small business, and labor.

Overall, the Federal Reserve System, with its component parts, attempts to keep close watch over the economy. The health of the economy greatly depends on number of jobs and consumer spending in the nation.

Monetary Policy

Monetary policy goals are outlined in the original *Federal Reserve Act*, signed more than 90 years ago by President Woodrow Wilson.[4] (A copy of the Act can be found on the Federal Financial Institutions Examination Council Web site, www.ffiec.gov/.)

Monetary policy has three goals:

1. To promote maximum employment
2. To achieve stable prices for goods, services, labor, and materials
3. To create moderate long-term interest rates

Long-term stable prices are a precondition for sustainable output, growth, and employment, as well as *moderate* long-term interest rates. The stable prices are undistorted by inflation and ultimately contribute to higher standards of living for Americans. In addition, stable prices foster *personal saving* because when the risk of erosion of assets is minimized, families are encouraged to save more. This is true for businesses as well, which are encouraged to invest more. In short, stability is essential for greater prosperity.

How Fed Policy Affects the Economy

The link between *policy* and the actual *economy* is the market for balances held at the Federal Reserve Banks. An easy way to see this is in the realization that literally hundreds of institutions have accounts at the Reserve Banks, and they *actively trade balances* held in these accounts. These trades are in the *federal funds market* and are conducted at an interest rate known as the *federal funds rate.* It is the Fed's control over the *federal funds rate,* through its influence over the *supply of* and *demand for* balances at the Reserve Banks, that drives the economy.

I know this can all seem rather confusing. However, what you have to understand is that the FOMC sets the rate at a level it believes will foster those financial and monetary conditions that will achieve its monetary policy objectives. A change in the federal funds rate can set off a chain of events that will affect other short-term interest rates, longer-term interest rates, the foreign exchange value of the dollar, and stock prices.

In a ripple effect, the changes in these variables will affect the spending decisions of individual households and businesses, which, in turn, affect the growth in aggregate demand and the economy.

Short-term interest rates, such as those on Treasury bills and commercial paper (unsecured, discounted, and negotiable notes sold by one company to another in order to satisfy immediate cash needs), are affected by the following:

- The current level of the federal funds rate
- Expectations about the overnight federal funds rate over the duration of the short-term contract

As a result, short-term interest rates may decline if the Federal Reserve reduces the federal funds rate or if events convince participants that the Federal Reserve will be holding the federal funds rate lower than had been anticipated. It is always interesting to watch Wall Street—and investors around the world—hold their collective breath when the Fed is due to announce its rate decision.

To that end, investors closely follow data releases and statements by Federal Reserve officials, searching for clues that the economy and prices are on a different trajectory than had been thought, which would have implications for the stance of monetary policy.

Changes in short-term interest rates can also influence *long-term* interest rates, such as those on Treasury notes, corporate bonds, fixed-rate mortgages, and other consumer loans. Those long-term rates are affected by the following:

- Changes in current short-term rates
- Expectations about short-term rates over the rest of the life of the long-term contract

Generally, economic news or statements by officials will have a greater impact on short-term interest rates than on longer rates. This is because they usually have a bearing on the course of both the economy and policy over a shorter period.

Changes in long-term interest rates also affect stock prices, which may have a noticeable effect on personal wealth. Lower interest rates may convince investors that the economy will be stronger and profits will be higher in the near future, which should further lift equity prices.

Changes in monetary policy also affect the *exchange value* of the dollar on currency markets. On the one hand, if interest rates rise in the United States, yields on dollar assets will look more favorable. This will lead to the *rise* of the dollar on foreign exchange markets. On the other hand, lower interest rates in the United States will cause a *decline* in the exchange value of the dollar. Both will affect the price of imports and exports with foreign nations.

Many other factors affect aggregate demand and supply, which, in turn, affect the economic position of households and businesses. On the demand side, the government influences the economy through changes in taxes and spending programs, which typically receive a lot of public attention and are therefore anticipated.

On the supply side, natural disasters, disruptions in crude oil delivery, agricultural losses, and slowdowns in productivity are examples of adverse supply shocks. Such shocks tend to *raise the prices* of goods and services.

Influences on Policy

Although the goals of monetary policy are quite clear and were set many years ago by the Federal Reserve Act, the actual ways to achieve those goals are often not so obvious, and the actions taken by the FOMC can take time to affect the economy. It is often far from obvious whether a selected level of the federal funds rate will achieve those goals. To understand the effects of fund rate decisions better, the Federal Reserve pays close attention to the following guides:

- Monetary aggregates
- The level and structure of interest rates
- The Taylor rule
- Foreign exchange rates

A brief discussion of each follows.

Monetary Aggregates   Monetary aggregates have a fairly stable relationship with the economy and can be controlled to a reasonable extent by the Federal Reserve, through control over either the supply of balances or the federal funds rate.

There are three monetary aggregates. According to the experts, the aggregates have had different roles in monetary policy as their reliability as guides has changed. Here is a list of their primary components:

Monetary Aggregate 1 (M1):

- Currency (and traveler's checks)
- Demand deposits
- NOW (*negotiable order of withdrawal*) and other interest-earning checking accounts

Monetary Aggregate 2 (M2):

- The three elements of M1
- Savings deposits and money market deposit accounts
- Small time deposits (time deposits in amounts of less than $100,000, excluding balances in IRA and Keogh accounts at depository institutions)
- Retail money market mutual fund balances (excluding balances held in IRA and Keogh accounts with money market mutual funds)

Monetary Aggregate 3 (M3):

- The elements of M2
- Large time deposits
- Institutional money market mutual fund balances
- Repurchase agreements
- Eurodollars

Interest Rates   Interest rates have frequently been proposed as a guide to policy because information on interest rates is available on a real-time basis. Those who argue against giving interest rates the primary role in guiding monetary policy are concerned with the uncertainty about exactly what level of interest is consistent with the basic goals of policy. Obviously, the best level of interest will vary, depending on the following circumstances.

- The stance of fiscal policy
- Changes in the pattern of household and business spending

- Productivity growth
- Economic developments abroad

That variance makes it difficult to gauge the strength of these forces and to translate them into a rational path for interest rates.

The Taylor Rule   It was John Taylor whose research prompted the proposal of what came to be called the Taylor rule, which states that the *real* short-term interest rate, *the interest rate adjusted for inflation,* should be determined according to three factors:

1. Where actual inflation is relative to the targeted level that the Fed wishes to achieve
2. How far economic activity is above or below its "full employment" level
3. What short-term interest rate is consistent with full employment

The rule recommends a relatively high interest rate, known as a *tight* monetary policy, when inflation is above its target *or* when the economy is above its full employment level. In opposite situations, the rule recommends a relatively low interest rate, known as an *easy* monetary policy. It was designed simply to provide recommendations for how a central bank such as the Federal Reserve should set short-term interest rates as economic conditions change to achieve both its short-term goal for stabilizing the economy and its long-term goal for fighting the inflation. The Fed does not always strictly follow the Taylor rule.[5]

Foreign Exchange Rates   Exchange rate movements are an important way through which monetary policy affects the economy. They tend to respond *promptly* to a change in the federal funds rate. Exchange rates, as well as the fed funds rate, are available continuously throughout the day.

However, sometimes the interpretation of those movements in exchange rates can be difficult. For example, a decline in the foreign exchange value of the dollar could indicate that monetary policy has become more accommodating, resulting in the risk of inflation.

Exchange rates respond to other influences as well, most notably political or social developments abroad. Thus, a weaker dollar on foreign exchange markets *could* reflect higher interest rates abroad, which make other currencies more attractive. Conversely, a strengthening of the dollar on foreign exchange markets could document a move to a more restrictive monetary policy in the United States. There is always the possibility that it could reflect expectations of a lower path for interest rates elsewhere or a heightened perception of risk in foreign financial assets relative to U.S. assets.

The role of foreign exchange rates in the formulation of monetary policy continues to be hotly debated by economists worldwide.

Implementation of Policy

U.S. monetary policy is implemented by affecting conditions in the market for balances that depository institutions hold at the Federal Reserve Banks. At one time, the FOMC sought to achieve *a specific quantity of balances*, but now it sets a target for the *interest rate* at which those balances are traded, the *federal funds rate*. It is implemented in a number of ways:

- Conducting open market operations
- Imposing reserve requirements
- Permitting depository institutions to hold contractual clearing balances
- Extending credit through its discount window facility

By these means, the Fed exercises considerable control over the demand for and supply of balances and the federal funds rate. Through its control of the federal funds rate, the Federal Reserve is able to foster financial and monetary conditions consistent with those three monetary policy objectives discussed earlier: the promotion of both *maximum employment* and *stable pricing for goods, services, labor, and materials,* as well as *the creation of moderate long-term interest rates.*

Federal Reserve, Contractual Clearing, and Excessive Reserve Balances   The Federal Reserve influences the economy through the market for *balances* that depository institutions maintain in their accounts at Federal Reserve Banks. The end-of-day balances in the various accounts of depository institutions are used to meet the balance requirements of the Federal Reserve.

If an institution ends the day with a large balance, it can reduce it in several ways, depending on how *long* it expects the surplus to persist. If it expects the surplus to be temporary, the institution can lend excess balances in financing *markets,* such as the market for *repurchase agreements* or the market for *federal funds.*

In the federal funds market, depository institutions actively trade balances held at the Federal Reserve *with each other,* usually overnight, on an uncollateralized basis. Basically, the banks with surplus balances lend them to other institutions that need larger balances.

You can see that the *federal funds rate,* the interest rate at which these transactions occur, is an *extremely* important benchmark in financial markets. Daily fluctuations in the federal funds rate reflect demand and supply conditions in the market for Federal Reserve balances.

There are three Federal Reserve balances to examine here: required reserve balances, contractual clearing balances, and excess reserve balances.

Required Reserve Balances   Required reserve balances are just that—balances that a depository institution *must* hold with the Federal Reserve.

Reserve requirements are imposed on all depository institutions, including commercial and savings banks, savings and loan associations, and credit unions. Reserve requirements are applied to *transaction* deposits, including *demand deposits* and *interest-bearing accounts* that offer unlimited checking privileges.

An institution's reserve requirement is just a *fraction* of such deposits, which is the *required reserve ratio,* a number set by the board of governors within limits prescribed in the Federal Reserve Act.

This requirement *expands or contracts* with the level of its transaction deposits and with the required reserve ratio set by the board. In practice, the changes reflect movements in transaction deposits because the Federal Reserve adjusts the required reserve ratio only infrequently.

A depository institution satisfies its reserve requirement by literally holding cash in its vault and by the balance maintained directly with a Federal Reserve Bank or indirectly with a correspondent bank. It is important to realize that it is the *difference* between an institution's reserve requirement and the *vault cash* used to meet that requirement that is called the *required reserve balance.* If the balance falls short of the reserve balance requirement, the shortfall may be subject to a fine.

Contractual Clearing Balances   Depository institutions also use their accounts at Federal Reserve Banks to *clear* many financial transactions. Given unpredictability of transactions that clear through a bank's accounts every day, they attempt to hold an *end-of-day* balance that is high enough to protect against unexpected debits that could leave their accounts overdrawn. If a depository institution finds that targeting an end-of-day balance equal to its required reserve balance provides insufficient protection against overdrafts, it may establish what is called a *contractual clearing balance,* sometimes called a *required clearing balance.*

This is an amount that a depository institution agrees to hold at its Reserve Bank *in addition* to any required reserve balance. In return, the bank earns interest, in the form of *earnings credits,* on the balance held to satisfy its contractual clearing balance. These credits are used to offset the cost of the Federal Reserve services it uses. Again, if the depository institution fails to satisfy its contractual requirement, it is subject to a charge. (It is similar to the overdraft fee your bank levies against your account when the balance is insufficient to cover your checks.)

Excess Reserve Balances   A depository institution may hold balances at its Federal Reserve Bank in addition to those it must hold to meet its reserve balance requirement and its contractual clearing balance; these balances are called *excess reserve balances,* or just *excess reserves.*

In most cases, institutions try to keep excess reserve balances *low,* because balances at the Federal Reserve do not earn interest. However, a depository institution may choose to hold some excess reserve balances as protection against an overnight overdraft in its account or the risk of failing to hold enough balances to satisfy the *reserve* or *clearing balance* requirements. This is the least-predictable component of the demand for balances.

Supply of Federal Reserve Balances   The supply of Federal Reserve balances comes from three sources:

1. The Federal Reserve's portfolio of securities and repurchase agreements
2. Loans from the Federal Reserve through its discount window facility
3. Autonomous factors

Let us examine them one by one.

Securities Portfolio   The *most* important source of balances to depository institutions is the Federal Reserve's *portfolio of securities.* That is fairly straightforward. The Federal Reserve buys and sells securities either on an outright *permanent* basis or *temporarily,* through *repurchase agreements* and *reverse repurchase agreements.*

These purchases or sales are called *open market operations,* essentially the Federal Reserve's *primary* means of influencing the supply of balances at the Federal Reserve Banks. They are conducted to align the supply of balances at the Federal Reserve with the demand for those balances at the target rate, which is set by the FOMC.

Purchasing securities *increases* the quantity of balances, while selling securities or conducting a reverse repurchase agreement *decreases* the quantity of Federal Reserve balances.

Discount Window Lending   The supply of Federal Reserve balances *increases* when banks borrow from the Federal Reserve's *discount window*. Access to discount window credit is established by rules set by the board of governors, and loans are made at interest rates set by the Reserve Banks and approved by the board.

The decision to borrow is based on the level of the lending rate and a bank's liquidity needs. The volume of balances supplied through the discount window is usually only a small portion of the total supply of Federal Reserve balances.

Autonomous Factors   The supply of balances can vary substantially because of movements in other factors, generally outside the Federal Reserve's direct control. The most important of these factors are *Federal Reserve notes, the Treasury's balance at the Federal Reserve,* and *Federal Reserve float.*

The Federal Reserve's conduct of *open market operations,* its *policies* related to required reserves and balances, and its *lending* through the discount window all play important roles in keeping the federal funds rate close to the FOMC's target rate.

Open market operations are the most powerful tool for controlling the funds rate. These operations, arranged nearly every business day, are designed to bring the supply of Federal Reserve balances in line with the demand for those balances at the FOMC's target rate.

Required balances facilitate the conduct of open market operations by creating a predictable demand for Federal Reserve balances. If the supply of balances falls short of demand, then discount window lending is the mechanism for *expanding* the supply of balances to contain pressures on the funds rate.

Reserve balance requirements and contractual clearing balances only need to be met on average over a *reserve maintenance period*, not every single day. This gives considerable flexibility to depository institutions to manage their end-of-day balances at the Federal Reserve from one day to the next, and helps smooth fluctuations in the federal funds rate.[6]

The Conduct of Open Market Operations

In theory, the Federal Reserve could conduct open market operations by purchasing or selling any type of asset, but most assets cannot be traded easily enough to accommodate open market operations.

For open market operations to work well, the Federal Reserve must be able to buy and sell *quickly*, whenever it chooses, and in whatever volume. These conditions require that the instrument it buys or sells be traded in a broad, highly active market that can accommodate the transactions without distortions or disruptions to the market itself.[7]

The U.S. Treasury securities market satisfies these conditions, as it is the broadest and most active of U.S. financial markets. The Federal Reserve Bank of New York conducts all open market operations for the Federal Reserve, under an authorization from the FOMC. The group that carries out the operations is commonly referred to as *the open market trading desk*, or *the desk* for short.

It is permitted to conduct business with U.S. securities dealers and with foreign official and international institutions that maintain accounts at the Federal Reserve Bank of New York. The dealers with which the desk transacts business are called *primary dealers*, and all transactions are conducted through an auction process.

Outright Sales and Purchases

The Federal Reserve conducts far more purchases than sales or redemptions of securities, primarily because it must offset the drain of balances resulting from the public's increasing demand for Federal Reserve notes.[8]

When the desk decides to buy securities, it determines how much it wants to buy. It then divides that amount into smaller portions, making a *series* of purchases in different segments of the maturity spectrum, rather than buying securities across all maturities at once, in order to minimize the impact on market prices.

When projections indicate a need to drain Federal Reserve balances, the desk may choose to *sell* or *redeem* maturing securities. However, the sale of securities is extremely rare.[9]

Repurchase and Reverse Repurchase Agreements

The Federal Reserve frequently arranges *repurchase agreements* to temporarily add Federal Reserve balances. In other words, it acquires a security from a primary dealer under an agreement to *return the security on a specified date.* Most such agreements have an overnight term, although short-term repurchase agreements with maturities of 2 to 13 days are also arranged to address shortages in Federal Reserve balances that are expected to extend over several days. There are longer-term repurchase agreements as well, which are used to address more persistent needs.[10]

When the Federal Reserve needs to *absorb* Federal Reserve balances temporarily, it enters into *reverse* repurchase agreements. These involve selling a Treasury security under an agreement to receive the security back on a specified date. As in repurchase agreement transactions, these operations are arranged on an auction basis.

The Federal Reserve also arranges reverse repurchase agreements with foreign official and international accounts at the Federal Reserve Bank of New York to help manage their U.S. dollar payments and receipts.[11]

In a nutshell, the Fed was designed to buy and sell securities, to maintain required balances in depository accounts, and to keep a watchful eye on current economic indicators.

Concluding Remarks

This appendix provided the basics of what you might like to know about the Federal Reserve System in relation to the Follow the Fed strategies. We do not want to overwhelm you with detail, but to give you an overview of the basic structure of the Fed and policy implementation processes involved in keeping the U.S. economy "on track." In other words, we want to give you just enough knowledge to use the Follow the Fed investing strategy confidently to build your personal wealth.

There is much more to learn about the Federal Reserve System, a wealth of information that may or may not be of interest to you. For those who wish to learn more, please visit one or more of the Web sites listed at the beginning of this appendix.

Glossary

The entries in this glossary are from a variety of sources, both Internet and traditional reference works.

asset manager   Another term for investment manager who handles investing funds, often in a portfolio of stocks.

bear market   When the stock market falls for a prolonged period of time, usually by 20 percent or more, and is characterized by widespread pessimism. It is the opposite of a *bull market.*

blue-chip company   A large, nationally recognized, well-established and financially sound company. Blue-chip companies are known to weather downturns and operate profitably in the face of an adverse economic condition, which helps to contribute to their long record of stable and reliable growth. The stock price of a blue chip usually closely follows the S&P 500.

book value   Net asset value of a company, which is its total assets minus liabilities.

bull market   Used to describe a prolonged period in which investment prices rise faster than their historical average. Bull markets can happen as a result of an economic recovery, an economic boom, or investor psychology. Bull markets tend to be associated with increased investor confidence. It is the opposite of a *bear market.*

buy and hold   A common long-term investment strategy, based on the belief that despite temporary ups and downs, the stock market will appreciate in the long term.

capital gain   The profit that results from the appreciation of a capital asset over its purchase price. The gain is not realized until the asset is sold. A capital gain may be short term (one year or less) or long term (more than one year) and must be declared for income tax purposes. A capital loss is incurred when there is a decrease in the capital asset value compared to its purchase price.

capitalization   Often called *market capitalization,* or *market cap,* this is a measurement of corporate or economic size equal to the share price times the number of shares outstanding of a public company. The investment community uses this figure to determining a company's size, as opposed to sales or total asset figures.

Depository Institutions and Monetary Control Act of 1980   A law passed under President Jimmy Carter, which gave the Federal Reserve greater control over non-member banks. Its main purpose was to compel all banks to adhere to the guidelines established by the Fed; the secondary purpose allowed credit unions and thrifts to offer checkable deposits.

DFA Micro-Cap   The mutual fund managed by Dimensional Fund Advisors dedicated to investing in micro-cap stocks. See www. dfaus.com for more details.

discounted cash flow (DCF)   Describes a method to estimate the attractiveness of an investment opportunity. Discounted cash flow (DCF) analysis uses free-cash-flow projections and discounts them to arrive at a present value. This is then used to evaluate the potential for investment. If the value arrived at through DCF analysis is higher than the current cost of the investment, the opportunity may be a good one.

discount window   This is a figurative expression for the Federal Reserve facility that extends credit directly to eligible depository institutions. This name derives from the early days of the Federal Reserve System when bankers would come to a Reserve Bank teller window to obtain credit.

Dow Jones Industrial Average (DJIA)   Also known as the Dow 30 or (informally) the Dow, this is one of several stock market indices created by *Wall Street Journal* editor Charles Dow in 1896. Originally, he compiled an index of 12 stocks. This has now grown to 30 of the largest and most publicly held companies.

enterprise value (EV)   A market value measure of a company from the aggregated point of view, incorporating all financial sources: debt holders, preferred shareholders, minority shareholders, and common equity holders.

exchange traded funds (ETFs)   ETFs represent a basket of stocks that reflect an index such as the S&P 500. An ETF, however, isn't a mutual fund; it trades just like any other company on a stock exchange.

exchange value   This term refers to one of four major attributes of a commodity—an item or service produced for, and sold on, the market. The other three aspects are *use value, value,* and *price.*

federal funds market   From day to day, the amount of reserves a bank wants to hold may change as its deposits and transactions change. When a bank needs additional reserves on a short-term basis, it can borrow them from other banks that happen to have more reserves than they need. These loans take place in a private financial market called the federal funds market.

federal funds rate   Rate charged by a depository institution on an overnight loan of federal funds to another depository institution; rate may vary from day to day and from bank to bank. It adjusts to balance the supply of and demand for reserves. For example, if the supply of reserves in the fed funds market is greater than the demand, then the funds rate falls, and if the supply of reserves is less than the demand, the funds rate rises.

Federal Reserve Act   This is the federal legislation, enacted in 1913 with the signature of President Woodrow Wilson, that established the Federal Reserve System.

Federal Reserve Bank   One of the 12 operating arms of the Federal Reserve System, located throughout the nation, that together with their branches carry out various System functions, including providing payment services to depository institutions, distributing the nation's currency and coin, supervising and regulating member banks and bank holding companies, and serving as fiscal agent for the U.S. government.

Federal Reserve District   One of the 12 U.S. geographic regions served by a Federal Reserve Bank.

Federal Reserve System   The central bank of the United States created by the Federal Reserve Act and made up of a seven-member Board of Governors in Washington, D.C., 12 regional Federal Reserve Banks, and Branches of the Federal Reserve Banks. It is often called the *Fed.*

Federal Open Market Committee (FOMC)   Sometimes just called *the committee,* this is a 12-voting-member committee made up of the seven members of the Board of Governors; the president of the Federal Reserve Bank of New York; and, on a rotating basis, the presidents of four other Reserve Banks. The FOMC generally meets eight times a year in Washington, D.C., to set the nation's monetary policy. It also establishes policy relating to the system's operations in the foreign exchange markets.

foreign exchange rate   The value of exchange between the U.S. dollar and foreign currencies, which is decided upon by the application of bilateral exchange formulas. For further information, see: www.federalreserve.gov/pubs/bulletin/2005/winter05_index.pdf.

growth stocks   Stocks that are considered expensive in terms of higher price/book, price/sales, or price/earnings ratios. Superior earnings growth prospects are often used to justify these higher ratios.

hedge fund   Usually an unregulated investment fund primarily for wealthy clients, often focusing on achieving absolute returns with reduced volatility.

index fund   Mutual fund that tracks a public index such as the S&P 500. Index funds are usually known for low costs of operation, including management fees.

initial public offering   An initial public offering, or IPO, is the first sale of stock by a company to the public.

interest rates   The percentage of a sum of money charged for its use. The rate can either be long-term or short-term, sometimes called the *short rate*; this is the interest rate charged for short-term transactions. This is in direct contrast to long-term rates where the transaction is in effect for a greater length of time.

Keogh plans   Pension plans for self-employed people. Sometimes they are called HR10 plans and are not individual retirement accounts (IRAs).

large capitalization stocks (large stocks)   Stocks of publicly traded companies that are in the upper range of market capitalizations, sometimes called *large-cap stocks*. This term is often used to refer to stocks in the S&P 500.

market capitalization   A stock term referring to a computation determined by multiplying the share price of a stock times the number of shares outstanding.

monetary aggregates   Aggregate measures through which the Federal Reserve monitors the nation's monetary assets: M1, M2, and M3.

M1   Measure of the U.S. money stock that consists of currency held by the public, traveler's checks, demand deposits, and other checkable deposits.

M2   Measure of the U.S. money stock that consists of M1, savings deposits (including money market deposit accounts), time deposits in amounts of less than $100,000, and balances in retail money market mutual funds. Excludes individual retirement accounts (IRAs) and Keogh balances at depository institutions and retail money funds.

M3   Measure of the U.S. money stock that consists of M2, time deposits of $100,000 or more at all depository institutions, repurchase agreements in amounts of $100,000 or more, Eurodollars, and balances held in institutional money market mutual funds.

monetary policy   The actions taken by the Federal Reserve System (or any central bank) to influence the availability and cost of money and credit, as a means of helping to promote national economic goals. Tools of monetary policy include open market operations, direct lending to depository institutions, and reserve requirements.

mutual fund   An open-ended fund operated by an investment company that raises money from shareholders and invests in a group of assets, in accordance with a stated set of objectives.

Nasdaq   National Association of Securities Dealers Automated Quotation System, a computerized system showing current bid and asked prices for stocks traded on the over-the-counter market, as well as some New York Stock Exchange listed stocks.

New York Stock Exchange   The largest and oldest stock exchange in the United States.

open market operations   Purchases and sales of securities, typically U.S. Treasury securities, in the open market, by the open market trading desk at the Federal Reserve Bank of New York as directed by the Federal Open Market Committee, to influence interest rates. Purchases increase the supply of Federal Reserve balances to depository institutions; sales do the opposite.

open market trading desk   The staff of the trading desk at the New York Federal Reserve Bank executes open market operations on behalf of the entire Federal Reserve System—uses their directives as a guide in making decisions about the day-to-day purchase or sale of securities.

price to book value (P/B ratio)   A ratio used to compare a stock's market value to its book value. It is calculated by dividing the current closing price of the stock by the latest quarter's book value per share.

$$P/B \; ratio \; = \; \frac{Share \; price}{Book \; value \; per \; share}$$

price to cash flow ratio (P/C ratio)   A measure of the market's expectations of a firm's future financial health. Since this measure deals with cash flow, the effects of depreciation and other noncash factors are removed.

$$P/C \; ratio = \frac{Share \; price}{Cash \; flow \; per \; share}$$

price to earnings ratio (P/E ratio) A valuation ratio of a company's current share price compared to its per-share earnings.

$$P/E \ ratio = \frac{Share \ price}{Earnings \ per \ share(EPS)}$$

price to sales ratio (P/S ratio) A ratio for valuing a stock relative to its own past performance, other companies, or the market itself. Price to sales is calculated by dividing a stock's current price by its revenue per share for the trailing 12 months. The ratio can also be referred to as a stock's PSR.

$$P/S \ ratio = \frac{Share \ price}{Revenue \ per \ share}$$

required reserve balance Money that a depository institution is required to maintain in the form of vault cash or, if vault cash is insufficient to meet the requirement, in the form of a balance maintained directly with a Reserve Bank or indirectly with a pass-through correspondent bank.

robber baron A negative term used to describe financial magnates of the nineteenth and early twentieth centuries who became wealthy through questionable means.

Russell Index A financial index managed by the Frank Russell Company, such as the Russell 2000. See www.russell.com for more details.

savings and loan association Historically, these were depository institutions that accepted deposits mainly from individuals and invested heavily in residential mortgage loans. Savings and loans now have many of the powers of commercial banks. Three institutions fall under the umbrella term *thrift institutions*: savings banks, savings and loan associations, and credit unions.

Securities Exchange Commission (SEC) A U.S. government agency responsible for enforcing the federal securities laws and regulating the stock market and securities industry.

small capitalization stocks (small stocks) Stocks of publicly traded companies that are in the lower range of market capitalization. This term is often used to refer to companies with a market capitalization of less than $1 billion, sometimes called small-cap stocks.

S&P 500 Stock index managed by Standard & Poor's of 500 of the largest stocks in terms of market capitalization in the United States.

Taylor's rule Taylor's rule is a formula developed by Stanford economist John Taylor, designed to provide recommendations for how a central bank like the Federal Reserve should set short-term interest rates as economic conditions change to achieve both its short-run goal for stabilizing the economy and its long-run goal for inflation.

thrift institutions Savings and loan associations and savings banks fall into the category of thrift institutions. Thrifts were originally established to promote personal savings through savings accounts and homeownership through mortgage lending, but now provide a range of services similar to many commercial banks.

Treasury bills One of three Treasury securities each considered an *obligation* of the U.S. government. They are issued by the U.S. Department of the Treasury as a means of borrowing money to meet government expenditures not covered by tax revenues. All marketable Treasury securities have a minimum purchase amount of $1,000 and are issued in $1,000 increments. The other marketable Treasury securities are *notes* and *bonds*.

value investing The strategy of selecting stocks that trade for less than their intrinsic value. Value investors actively seek stocks of companies that they believe the market has undervalued.

value stock Stocks that are considered cheap in terms of lower price/book, price/sales, or price/earnings ratios.

whipsaws A term defining a situation where a trader takes a position, and then has to counter that to stop loss limits and liquidation of position—and then has to move back in the original direction. Usually seen during periods of volatility in the market.

Notes

Chapter 2

1. www.investopedia.com/terms/l/leveragedbuyout.asp.

Chapter 3

1. Frederic Morton, *The Rothschilds, A Family Portrait* (New York: Atheneum, 1962).

2. Bouck White, *The Book of Daniel Drew: A Glimpse of the Fisk-Gould-Tweed Regime from the Inside* (New York: Doubleday, Page and Company, 1910). Reprinted by the American Research Council in 1965.

Chapter 4

1. Sidney Ratner, James H. Soltow, and Richard Sylla, *The Evolution of the American Economy: Growth, Welfare, and Decision Making* (New York: Macmillan Publishing, 1993).

2. Sean Wilentz, *The Rise of American Democracy: Jefferson to Lincoln,* (New York: W. W. Norton, 2005).

Chapter 6

1. Jack Bogle, "As the Index Fund Moves from Heresy to Dogma . . . What More Do We Need to Know?" Speech, April 13, 2004. www.vanguard.com/bogle_site/sp20040413.html.

2. http://money.cnn.com/2007/08/03/news/international/carlosslim.fortune/index.htm

Chapter 7

1. Jeremy Siegel, *Stocks for the Long Run* (New York: McGraw-Hill, 2002), p. 349.

2. Paul Mladjenovic, *Stock Investing for Dummies* (Hoboken, NJ: John Wiley & Sons, 2002), p. 15.

3. A History of Standard and Poors, retrieved from http://www2 .standardandpoors.com/spf/html/media/SP_TimeLine_ 2006.html. Summer, 2007.

4. Mladjenovic, p. 15.

5. Siegel, p. 132.

6. Bogle Financial Markets Research Center, "The Gary M. Brinson Distinguished Lecture," The Index Fund Moves from Heresy to Dogma . . . What More Do We Need to Know? By John C. Bogle, Washington State University, Pullman, Washington, April 13, 2004, www.vanguard.com.

Chapter 8

1. Martin E. Zweig, *Martin Zweig's Winning on Wall Street* (New York: Warner Books, 1986), pp. 35, 40.

2. Paul Mladjenovic, *Stock Investing for Dummies* (Hoboken, NJ: John Wiley & Sons, 2002), p. 195.

3. Ibid.

4. Jeremy Siegel, *Stocks for the Long Run* (New York: McGraw-Hill, 2002), p. 134.

5. David Dreman, *Contrarian Investment Strategies: The Next Generation,* (Simon & Schuster, 1998), p. 319.

6 Ibid.

Chapter 9

1. Martin Mayer, *The Fed* (New York: First Plume Printing, 2002), p. 74.

2. Charles R. Geisst, *100 Years of Wall Street* (New York: McGraw-Hill, 2000), p. 64.

Appendix

1. Board of Governors of the Federal Reserve System, *The Federal Reserve System*, 9th ed. (Washington, D.C.: U.S. Government Printing Office, 2005), p. 3.

2. Ibid., p. 2.

3. Ibid., p. 11.

4. Ibid., p. 2.

5. Ibid., pp. 23–24.

6. Ibid., p. 35.

7. Ibid., p. 36.

8. Ibid., p. 38.

9. Ibid., p. 39.

10. Ibid., p. 39.

11. Ibid., p. 40.

About the Author

Douglas S. Roberts is the Founder and Chief Investment Strategist for the Channel Capital Research Institute. He is a contributor to AOL's Money & Finance section and is frequently called on by the media as an expert on the Federal Reserve. His comments appear regularly on CNN/Money, MarketWatch.com, theStreet.com, Reuters, and the Dow Jones Newswires, and he appears frequently on CNBC and Fox Business News.

Doug was a vice president and portfolio manager at Bernstein Investment Management and Research, a unit of Alliance Capital Management, L.P., from 1999 to 2001. In addition to his portfolio management responsibilities, he led his group's strategies, focusing on quantitative investment analysis and sector allocation, as well as the evaluation of alternative asset investment vehicles.

From 1994 to 1998, Doug was a managing director of the Roberts Mitani Group, a New York merchant bank specializing in the investment of capital from Japan and East Asia. From 1992 to 1994, he served as a founding member of the board of directors of Benson Eyecare Corporation, which had been listed on the American Stock Exchange prior to its sale.

From 1985 to 1992, Doug was the chief operating officer of the Flori Roberts/Dermablend Group, a family-owned pharmaceutical/cosmetic group of companies that was acquired for $22 million in cash and stock by IVAX Corporation (IVX-ASE) in 1992. Subsequent to the acquisition, he served as Chief Operating Officer of the Personal Care Products Group and assistant to the Chairman–Special Projects from 1992 to 1994.

Doug began his career as an associate of the Morgan Stanley Group, working in the corporate finance department in both the New York and London offices from 1983 to 1985. He earned a BS and an MBA from the Wharton School at the University of Pennsylvania in 1983.

He serves on the international board of governors of Sigma Phi Epsilon fraternity and the board of trustees of the Ranney School and is a member of the Explorers Club for his participation in the discovery of the *U-869*, a World War II German submarine, off the coast of New Jersey, as featured in the book, *Shadow Divers*. He holds a second-degree black belt in the Imperial system of tae kwon do. Doug is married with two children.

Index

A

Acquisition costs, 22
Active trading, 78
Advisory committees, of Federal
    Reserve System, 161–62
The Age of Turbulence
    (Greenspan), 108
Aldrich, Nelson, 48
American Express, 37
America Online (AOL), 79
Anheuser-Busch, 37
Annualized rate, 119
Automobile industry, Internet
    versus, 38
Average equity funds, 16, 90
Avon Products, 37

B

Banking
    authority, 60
    central, 44–47
    failures, 50
    interests, 39
    Morgan and, 40
    national system, 48
    reforms, 42, 43
    Rothschild family and,
        39–40
Bank of England, 45
Bankruptcy, 23, 47, 155
Banks, member, 157
Banz, Rolf, 80
Bear market
    of 1973–1974, 38
    defined, 34

drawdowns in, 87–90, 97
Berkshire Hathaway, 29, 30,
    58, 67
Black & Decker, 37
Black Monday, 88
Black Tuesday, 88
Blue-chip companies, 91
Board of governors, of Federal
    Reserve System, 157–58
Bogle, Jack, 16, 17, 66, 75, 83, 84,
    90, 94
Bogle Financial Markets Research
    Center, 15
Book-to-market, 82
Book value, 29
Booth, David, 84
Bristol-Myers, 37
Brokerage
    commissions, 76
    costs, 135
    fees, 10, 138
    hedge funds and, 24
Bryan, William Jennings, 48
Buffett, Warren, 26, 27, 58, 67, 70,
    71, 78, 79, 98, 137
Buffett millionaires
    defined, 28–29
    revelations of, 28–30
Bull market, 30, 52
    defined, 34
Business portfolio, 15
Buy and hold growth
    stocks, 37
Buy and hold strategy, 53, 55,
    76–77, 78, 111, 116
    problem with, 54